# The Rhythm for Life

Praise for Les Snowdon's previous books:

## The Walking Diet

'Forget jogging, the gym and weight training. Walking is the easiest, cheapest, most convenient and effective exercise of all. *The Walking Diet* ends calorie counting . . . follow the easy food rules and the pounds will fall away even faster.'
*Daily Express*

'It makes you slim and is the antidote to stress, nervous tension and depression. What's more, it doesn't cost anything and everyone can do it.'
*Scotland on Sunday*

## Fitness Walking

'*The Walking Diet* proved a godsend to those of us who had been seduced into thinking exercise could only work if it hurt and cost a lot of time and money. Twelve months on, the authors have come up with *Fitness Walking* . . . the safest, cheapest and easiest way of losing weight, beating stress and improving your health.'
*Daily Express*

## Walk Slim: The Easy Way to Lose a Stone in 30 Days

'. . . Then it happened. On to my desk dropped a book which promised a *new life*. I am hooked. It doesn't involve expensive equipment, no stress on joints, neither do you have to get a second mortgage to join some exclusive health club. So what is the secret? What is it that promises to shed pounds painlessly? Walking.'
*The Herald*

'*Walk Slim* is the fat-free way to get fit. A calorie-burning pastime that can help get back some of what our increasingly sedentary lifestyles are taking away . . . The secret is in its simplicity.'
*Evening Mail*

# The
# Rhythm
# for Life

## Seven Highly Effective Ways
## to Walk Away from Stress

## LES SNOWDON

MAINSTREAM
PUBLISHING

EDINBURGH AND LONDON

First published in Great Britain in 1998 by
MAINSTREAM PUBLISHING COMPANY (EDINBURGH) LTD
7 Albany Street
Edinburgh EH1 3UG

ISBN 1 84018 049 8

A catalogue record for this book is available from the British Library

Typeset in Bembo and Sanvito Light
Printed and bound in Great Britain by The Cromwell Press Ltd

If you are unfit, pregnant, or have a diagnosed medical problem which will
affect your ability to exercise, you should check with your doctor before
commencing a vigorous exercise programme. The author and publishers cannot
accept responsibility for any injury or damage suffered as a result of attempting
an exercise in this book.

*To Maggie with love*

# Contents

# Acknowledgements

I would like to thank Maggie Humphreys for her support, inspiration and painstaking work in creating the stress-free diet and recipes; Sandra Sheffield, Fitness and Exercise Cert., SKFA, for the exercise routines; and Irene Barry and Sue Sharples for the illustrations.

# Foreword

*'A slow sort of country!' said the Queen. 'Now here, you see, it takes all the running you can do, to keep in one place. If you want to get somewhere else, you must run at least twice as fast as that!'*

Lewis Carroll in *Through the Looking Glass* reflected the problems of many of us in contemporary society. The pace and stress of life is more frenetic than ever before, with people not spending enough time reflecting on their lifestyle: exercise, eating the right foods, balancing home and work, and looking after their own and their family's health and well-being. 'Stress' is now as much a part of our modern vocabulary as laptops, fast food and e-mail. In this book, Les Snowdon helps you to think through your day-to-day lifestyle, and he motivates you to reflect on the current 'rhythm of your life' – how exercise, diet and relaxation techniques can help you take control of your life and turn stress into motivation and inspiration.

Cary L. Cooper
Professor of Organisational Psychology
Pro-Vice Chancellor (External Activities)
University of Manchester
Institute of Science and Technology

# PART ONE

# Awareness

*In the beginning was rhythm.*
HANS VON BULOW

*The same stream of life that runs*
*through my veins night and day runs*
*through the world and dances*
*in rhythmic measures.*
RABINDRANATH TAGORE, *SONG OFFERINGS*

# The First Way – In Step with your Daily Rhythms

*The world is too much with us: late and soon*
*Getting and spending, we lay waste our powers:*
*Little we see in nature that is ours . . .*
*For this, for every thing, we are out of tune.*
WILLIAM WORDSWORTH

What does it mean to be 'out of tune'?

You know what it feels like. You get up in the morning . . . you haven't slept well, you're edgy, you're thinking ahead to events during the day which you'd rather put off. Then you hurry breakfast and join the rest of the rat race rushing to the office or factory; or perhaps you are busy getting children off to school and trying to balance the conflicting interests of running a home and doing a job. Or you're retired, and you're anxious about money or about how you're going to spend your time. You're already showing the first signs of stress – you're out of tune with your own mind and body rhythms.

The poet Wordsworth wrote the above lines in the early years of the nineteenth century, when the Industrial Revolution in Britain was only 30 years old. Yet even then, the visionary Wordsworth could see men and women harnessed to the plough of the new industrial and consumer society – a society which would dominate the world during the next 200 years. And his observation then, as no doubt it would be now if he were still alive, is that 'we are out of tune'.

# Are You Under Stress?

From the moment we wake to the moment our head touches the pillow at night, most of us are tuned in to the vibrations happening all around us – radio, television, the stereo, the car radio, pop music, muzak. And noise – endless noise grinding out its frenzied message through our minds and bodies all day long. Traffic noise, aircraft noise, office noise – and noisy people, noisy neighbours, noisy children. Environmental pollution, and social pollution – aggressive behaviour, harassment and bullying.

And there's inner noise. The incessant voice-over in our minds. Many of us don't live in the present. We don't live in the moment, in the NOW. We are always thinking ahead to what we are going to do next. Our lives stretch before us in an endless whirl of things to do, places to go, people to see.

There are endless visual images for our minds to process. From the day we are born we are programmed to be consumers. Our minds are bombarded with endless sales chatter and images. It has been estimated that the average person has seen 40–50 million advertisements by the age of 60.

And there's the face we have to present to the world each morning through the guise of our persona. Dr Hans Selye, who wrote *The Stress of Life*, said: 'Most of our tensions and frustrations stem from the compulsive need to act out the role of someone we are not.' Pushed by rush, much of the time we act out roles allotted to us by others. We don't know why. We've been doing it for so long, we can't remember. We don't stop to think, because we have no time to think. Is it any wonder that for many of us life appears to be no more than a daily grind with little hope of change?

In 1996, The Institute of Management estimated that between 50 and 60 million working days are lost each year through stress, with a cost to the UK of about £7 billion. And the figure could be much higher if regular absences for complaints such as colds and migraines are taken into account. This represents a massive 500 per cent increase in lost working days since the 1950s, when life's pace was much more gentle. In a TUC survey, also in 1996, stress was reported as the major hazard for staff in 68 per cent of firms employing more than 1,000 employees. In smaller firms, 73 per cent of employees were found to be afflicted by excessive stress.

Technology makes it more and more difficult to get away from it all, even on holiday. You can take your mobile phone with you, you can take your laptop computer, or you can be contacted by e-mail and collect your mail at a virtual post office anywhere in the world. Connected by an invisible umbilical cord to the information superhighway, you are always on call. Somebody is always waiting to talk to you. Something is always urgent.

## What Is Stress?

Stress – mental, emotional or physical strain or tension – has always played a part in our lives. Whether it's stress at work, stress at home, stress in commuting or stress in relationships, most of us, at some time or another, know what it feels like to be under stress.

A little bit of stress is good for you. It helps you to be more alert, sharper and more motivated. But it can be harmful when your health is constantly placed under a high level of unrelieved tension and anxiety. The negative effects of stress have far-reaching consequences that go well beyond the individual.

In the '80s, we were told that we were approaching the age of leisure. We would all work fewer hours, we would share jobs, we would embrace teleworking, and we would spend more time with our families and savour the fruits of our labours. As we all know, for those left in work, the age of leisure has passed us by. Fewer people are working longer hours to keep the industrial and commercial machine running. And they are paying the price.

Cary Cooper, professor of organisational psychology at the University of Manchester Institute for Science and Technology, deplores the 'long-hours work culture', calling it 'presenteeism' – the competitive office atmosphere where employees stay on late because they are terrified of being the first to leave. He says: 'Between being at work, travelling to and from work, business travelling and thinking about work, some people have no life outside.'

Long hours alone may not make people ill, but they can increase health risks such as lack of exercise, increased smoking and drinking, and poor eating habits. Stress destroys essential vitamins and minerals and lowers the body's immune system. It can trigger high blood pressure and fatigue and it can cause biochemical changes in our bodies which, if left unchecked, can lead to cancer, heart disease and other illnesses.

There was a time when life was much simpler for humans. If attacked, we would either fight or run away – the 'fight or flight' reaction. If we needed food, we hunted or perished. If our bodies couldn't cope with stress, we died. Only the fittest survived. But our bodies are thousands of years out of date with our lifestyles.

Stress is not unique to the UK. It is a phenomenon of the western world and a western lifestyle. In the United States, the annual cost of job-related stress is estimated at more than $200 billion. A review by two American stress researchers who looked at a number of studies of life stress – occupational or otherwise – concluded that around 25 per cent of the population was chronically stressed.

Dr Hans Selye said: 'Stress is part of life. It is a natural by-product of all our activities. There is no more justification for avoiding stress than for shunning food, exercise or love.' Handled positively, stress can recharge and stimulate you into taking control of your life. By learning to turn stress into inspiration and motivation, you can be fitter and healthier, more creative and better organised, and you can communicate more effectively and assertively.

Stress is the 'dis-ease' of the modern age. It's an early warning signal, telling us that we are not 'in control of our lives' and that we need to take action.

## Recognising the Early Warning Signals

Consider what happened to Susan, Jack, Karen and Michael when they were exposed to high levels of stress in their lives:

**Susan** was a single mother and a primary school teacher. She worried that she didn't spend as much time as she should with her three-year-old daughter Katie. Time was passing so quickly and the precious years of Katie's childhood would soon be over. To make matters worse, Susan's school had recently been severely criticised by the Local Education Authority for its poor educational standards. This had caused conflict within the school and with parents. The teaching staff had been advised that the school would be reorganised and there would be redundancies. One teacher had already taken early retirement after suffering a complete nervous breakdown, and two other teachers were on extended sick leave.

This had meant Susan having to cope with an increased workload and additional activities after school. She felt that she was a good teacher, and she loved the children, but she had little confidence in herself and feared she might lose her job. Her friends told her to be more assertive, but it wasn't in Susan's nature to push herself forward. She suffered constant stomachaches and migraines and she rarely got a full night's sleep. 'What's wrong with me?' she asked herself as she lay awake at night. The only relief she got was in looking forward to the long holidays at the end of term.

**Jack** was a middle-aged marketing manager working for a large multinational computer corporation. His work took him all over the world and he rarely spent more than a fortnight at a time in the office where he was based. Jack's wife, Mary, said that he was always in a hurry and he should relax more. But that's not Jack. Jack was often doing three things at once. He would skip his lunch hour and use the time to catch up on phone calls, eat a sandwich and read a marketing report. Jack had always been a go-getter, a high-flyer. He said that being aggressive, competitive and ambitious went with the territory. But his work and lifestyle were starting to take their toll on Jack's family. Mary said that he was rarely at home and when he was at home, he was always working. Not for the first time, his wife had threatened to leave him and take the children with her. It would have devastated Jack. He loved Mary and the kids, and he couldn't understand why she got so upset. He worked hard and he was a good provider, wasn't he? But these days he was increasingly edgy, always snapping at everybody, and he was smoking and drinking more than usual to compensate. Jack never stopped to think and reflect on his relationship with Mary and the family and where his life was taking him. They were always arguing, even in bed, and he couldn't see an end to his problems.

**Karen** was a housewife. Looking after a three-year-old, with two children at school, she complained that she had little time to exercise and keep fit. She had always had a weight problem. Karen's husband, Nick, was forever asking her to exercise and eat more healthily. She did try aerobics classes with a friend, and Nick bought her an exercise bike. But her enthusiasm was always short-lived. In contrast, Nick went to the gym regularly and worked out, and he played squash once a week with his friend Tony. Karen continued to pile on the weight. She was a chocoholic and she binged all day on snacks. Nick had noticed that two of the children were starting to mirror their mother's eating habits, and he was worried that they would grow up to be overweight like her. He'd also noticed that Karen was spending a lot of her day watching television and neglecting the housework. Nick would come in some nights and find the dirty dishes still in the sink. Then he'd get angry and they'd argue in front of the kids. It was getting them both down. Karen wanted to lose weight, she knew that she was spending too much time watching television, and she was concerned that the children were beginning to suffer. But she was caught in a vicious circle. The more she tried, the more she failed and the more depressed she became, until the doctor had to prescribe anti-depressants for her to get through the day.

**Michael** was in his late fifties and was retired. His company was downsizing and restructuring, so he was given three months' notice and a redundancy payment to compensate him for his 35 years' service to the company. Michael had always been a loyal employee and over the years his dedication had been rewarded with two Employee Achievement Awards for making suggestions for improvements in productivity. His last award, two years ago, was presented to him personally by Sam Wise, the company's Group Managing Director. While some men his age look forward to retirement, Michael is still smarting from his brusque dismissal from the company he loved. He feels angry and resentful towards some of the colleagues he left behind who have replaced him: 'University graduates! Wet behind the ears. They can't spell, they can't add up without a calculator, and they're always taking time off sick.' Michael is still angry. He suffers bouts of depression and he recently suffered a mild heart attack which shocked both him and his family. His doctor advised him to make an effort to let go of the past, find some new interests to occupy his time, and get out and exercise more.

Do you recognise yourself in any of these stressed souls? Is there just a little bit of Susan, Jack, Karen and Michael in all of us? A number of surveys have found that stress is often linked to situations beyond an individual's control. Neither Susan, Jack,

Karen nor Michael could see a way out of their problems, and it took its toll on their health and their relationships with others. They all felt that events were running out of control and life was grinding them down.

We are all influenced by events, and like sleepwalkers we rush headlong into the future. Tense, anxious, overworked, uncertain and confused, we lack the insight to repair our tired minds and bodies. But it doesn't have to be like that. We should remember that we always have a choice. As Vance Packard, author of *The Hidden Persuaders*, said: 'We can choose not to be persuaded.' And we can choose not to be stressed; we can choose not to be manipulated and bullied; we can choose a different role to play; we can choose a simpler lifestyle – we can choose to delay those household purchases or that new car we were hankering after. We can choose to take things a little easier, let go a little, reflect more . . . and stand and stare . . . and wake up to our own awareness. We can choose to get in touch with our own inner rhythms.

## Fascinating Rhythm

*He who possesses rhythm possesses the universe.*
CHARLES OLSON, POET

Rhythm is connected with the most primitive and deeply ingrained impulses in our nature. Rhythm comes from a Greek word meaning 'flow', which means movement from one point to another. Water flows along river beds; crowds flow along city streets; blood flows in our veins. The beating of our hearts and the regular inhalation and exhalation of our breathing are the two most basic rhythms in our lives. When these movements cease, we are dead. Rhythm runs through our very nature and we are conditioned to respond to it even before we are born. A baby in the womb both feels and hears its mother's heartbeat and senses the regular sound of her breathing. Then, when it is born, rhythm soothes the newborn child, as it is rocked gently to comfort it, and songs and lullabies are sung to send it to sleep.

As a baby grows, one of the first things it wants to do is to walk. After crawling around on all fours, suddenly the rhythmic footfall of walking on two legs – left-right-left-right, one-two-one-two –

confers a sense of order and freedom and opens up a new world of opportunity. As rhythmical beings, walking is one of the first things we want to do; and it is one of the last things we want to give up.

The rhythms of our bodies are in turn paralleled by the slower rhythms of nature – night and day, summer and winter, heat and cold, storm and calm. All the movements in the universe, from the smallest atom to the largest star, vibrate in rhythm. All life is rhythmical and rhythm is life.

There is a creative force, power and energy that exists in rhythm, helping us to tap into our inherent natural rhythms for health and harmony. The healing power of rhythm can recharge our physical and mental batteries; it can unlock destructive emotions and create harmony out of disorder. The philosopher Plato said: 'Rhythm sinks deep into the recesses of the soul and takes the deepest hold there, bringing grace of body and mind.' When we are stressed and 'out of tune', and life seems just too much for us, we can tap into these natural rhythms by cultivating awareness and a sense of balance in our life.

One of the major factors that determines how you start the day – whether you feel relaxed, alert and cheerful, or sluggish, irritable and unable to concentrate – is your 'circadian rhythms'. These are a set of biological fluctuations which regulate sleep, hunger, cardiovascular activity, mood and body temperature. Your body temperature, for example, normally drops as you sleep and in most people hits a low period between 3 a.m. and 5 a.m. The heart rate is down and certain hormone levels are depressed. During the day, as your body temperature rises, your mood rises with it, and your alertness and ability to perform rise as well.

Body rhythms can be affected by factors such as food, drink, drugs and staying up late. But you can influence these natural rhythms. One of the most efficient ways is to elevate your deep body temperature, and the easiest way to do that is to exercise. Your body is not built for sitting around – it is built for movement.

Awareness begins with the body. You were born to move – your body, your heart, your mind and your spirit. This is what recreation means: re-creation, putting you back together, connecting you with your inner rhythms, making you whole.

# Body Awareness – Shape up for Life

Much of the time our bodies are sluggish, and our blood never gets an airing. Oxygen is rarely allowed to surge through our veins making us feel energetic, alive and vital. But exercise can change all that. It rejuvenates and revitalises the body's cells, releasing muscular tension and replenishing our energy levels. Exercise motivates, energises and empowers. 'The easiest way to change yourself is physically,' says American fitness expert Dr George Sheehan. 'Physical change is quick.' So kick-start your day with these wake-up stretches. They will tone and energise you, and connect you with your inner rhythms.

# Morning Energiser – Get up and Go

*Shoulder shrugs*

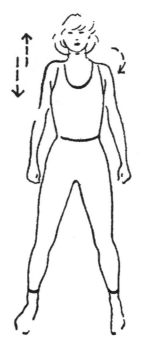

Loosens and relaxes the neck, shoulders and upper back. Stand upright with knees slightly bent, pelvis tucked under, back straight and abdominals pulled in (i.e. pelvic tilt). Relax arms down by your sides. Lift one shoulder up towards your earlobe, then relax down. Repeat alternating shoulders, 6–8 counts each side. Then rotate both shoulders back slowly 8 times, then forward slowly 8 times, drawing large circles.

*Upward stretch*

Lengthens muscles of upper back, arms and sides of body. Standing as before, raise arms above head, reaching up and holding 4 counts, then relax arms down by sides. Repeat 3 times. Convert to a waist stretch by following above, then, with arms above head, reach upwards with one arm as high as you can (lifting up and out of waist) while gently pulling the opposite shoulder down. Hold 4 counts. Relax, then repeat on other side.

*Shoulder/upper back stretch*

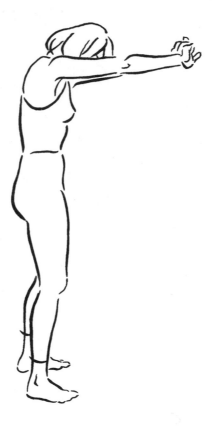

Standing as before (pelvic tilt), relax chin down towards chest (to relax and lengthen back of neck), place one hand on top of the other and press palms forward, separating shoulder blades and so opening across upper back. Hold 6–8 counts. Relax and repeat.

*Chest stretch*

Standing as above, relax shoulders down, clasp hands behind back, squeeze shoulder blades together and slowly lengthen and lift arms up and back. Hold 6 counts, relax and repeat.

*Lower back stretch*

Place hands on to thighs and bend knees with feet slightly wider than shoulder width apart. Pull abdominals in and tuck bottom right under, rounding the lower back. Hold 8 counts. Relax.

# Evening Nerve Soother – Breathe and Relax

At the end of the day, this deep relaxation soother will help you relax and unwind, and it will replenish vital energy lost during the day through physical, mental or emotional exertion. Lie flat on the floor in the 'corpse' position, with or without a pillow under your head, your hands by your sides, palms facing the ceiling. Let your feet relax, and either let your head sink into the pillow or roll it to one side. Then close your eyes, and get in touch with the rhythm of your breath. Relax. Breathe deeply and rhythmically from the abdomen for 20 minutes. Concentrate on raising your abdomen as you inhale, filling your lower, mid and upper lungs with air. Deep breathing balances the energies and focuses the mind, and it acts like a tranquilliser, calming the nervous system. It helps you tap into and follow the natural rhythms of breath and heartbeat.

A variation on deep relaxation is 'progressive relaxation'. Progressive relaxation is a method developed by an American doctor, Edmund Jacobson, in about 1910. It involves recognising tension and then letting go of it step by step – by progressively contracting and relaxing each of the body's muscles. You simply ask your neck to relax, and it relaxes. Ask your shoulder to relax, and it relaxes; ask your leg to relax, and it relaxes.

Either lie on the floor as before or sit in a comfortable chair. Close your eyes and breathe normally.

- Begin with your toes. Contract the muscles in your toes and hold for five seconds. Release and feel all the tension draining out of the muscles.
- Move up to your feet and ankles. Contract the muscles, hold for five seconds and release.
- Repeat method by moving up to the lower legs (front), lower legs (rear), knees, thighs, hips, buttocks, abdomen, lower back, upper back, chest, hands, arms, shoulders, neck, back of head, top of head, forehead, jaw and facial muscles.
- When you have finished the sequence, remain still and bask awhile in this state of complete relaxation.

As you wake up to your own awareness and learn to ride the wave of your inner rhythms, you will begin to feel less stressed, more relaxed, more confident and more in control of your life.

# PART TWO

# Renewal

*I got rhythm.*
IRA GERSHWIN

*It don't mean a thing*
*If it ain't got that swing.*
DUKE ELLINGTON AND IRVING MILLS

# The Second Way – Step away from Stress

*What do we see in a person's walk? . . .*
*we see everything, the whole biography.*
TED HUGHES, POET LAUREATE

Next time you walk along the street, look at the people walking towards you – really look at them, and study them. What do you see? Relaxed, happy faces; or furrowed brows and troubled faces? And how do they walk? With brisk, purposeful steps, with eyes looking straight ahead; or with short, shuffling steps, head down, gazing at nothing in particular?

The way you walk affects your mood; the way you walk affects your body, mind and spirit. To reduce stress in your life you need to relax. And the quickest way to relax is to walk with a positive, rhythmic movement. When inner tension builds, holding it in can lead to depression and, eventually, physical symptoms. Walking works like a safety valve to detox the build-up of these inner pressures. Walking decreases stress hormones and increases relaxation hormones (beta-endorphins) which elevate your mood and increase your sense of well-being: the 'walker's high'.

Walking is a natural mood-elevator. It helps promote feelings of happiness and it can ease mild depression. Walking gets you going, revs up your circulation and gives you the energy to get through the day. So put some glow, sparkle, pizzazz and WOW! back into your life. Smile more at the people you meet along the way and make the world a happier, more friendly place.

Walking is the quickest way to develop a sense of rhythm in your life. The alternating rhythmic motion of the arms and legs is similar to the inhalation and exhalation of the lungs when you breathe. So walk, let go, and surrender to your own natural rhythms – to the beat of your heart, the wave of your breath and the sound of your own inner music. Walking restores a sense of balance which counteracts the harmful effects of cumulative stress. As you walk, your feet feel the pulse of the earth below you and your body 'feels' the rhythm, becomes the rhythm, and you become involved in a process, a flow, like a river. It's this flow experience – the flow of breath, the flow of the body, the flow of air around you – that slows and stills the mind and spirit. The smooth rhythmic swing of the arms back and forth has a meditational effect on the mind similar to Zen and transcendental meditation.

So make time for yourself today. Go for a walk – and lift your head higher, walk tall and look around you. On foot you make the time to see things whole. Savour the sights, sounds and smells of the journey. Touch the air around you and touch your own peace. Make friends with yourself and the world around you and think pleasant thoughts, and your problems will just dissolve away.

## Walking – Today's Smart Stress-buster

The human body is the ultimate exercise machine, and walking is the easiest and safest way for most people to re-energise their bodies and burn away the harmful effects of stress, in other words, to experience health, fitness and deep relaxation. Anyone can walk. Whether you're lean and fit or 20 pounds overweight, you can reap walking's amazing benefits immediately.

To get into the habit of walking so that it becomes second nature to you, get up this very moment and go for a walk. Right now (assuming you're not reading this at 30,000 feet or in the middle of the night). Put the book down, get up and go for a walk. Any walk; around the block where you live or work, around the local park – anywhere. As long as it is close to you and easy to get to. How far and how fast you walk isn't important. All that matters is that you walk, and put out of mind any thoughts that are troubling you. Just empty your mind and walk. Don't worry if some of the thoughts keep coming back to bug you. Just note their presence and let them go on their way.

Feel better? What did you notice? That just moving and letting go can give you a tremendous feeling of physical and mental release? There is good reason for it. Action absorbs anxiety. Something as simple as the rhythmic action of walking can take you out of yourself and give you an immediate uplift. When you read a book, you are thinking – using the conscious mind. When you get up and walk in a relaxed, mindful way, you step aside from the conscious mind and become 'centred within yourself'. You suspend conscious thought for a time, and just go with the flow and rhythm of the walk.

Well, that's only the beginning. There's a lot more to walking than a walk around the block, but it's a start – and, as the Chinese say, a journey of a thousand miles begins with just one step.

## Make a 30-Day Commitment

Starting Monday (you can begin any day of the week, but Monday is a good day to make a new start), step out and follow the 30-day stress-release plan. You will notice that if you make Monday your first day, every sixth and seventh day correspond with a weekend, and activities are included which will help you wind down and prepare for the following week.

If you've been sedentary for some time and are generally unfit, then begin walking at your normal pace for a few days, then increase speed gradually to a brisk, aerobic pace between 3.5 and 4 mph. An easy way to measure walking speed is to work out your stride length and calculate how many steps you take each minute (see over the page). This calculates your speed based on three common stride lengths.

The only equipment you need is a pair of well-cushioned shoes that give good support. The only caution is that you should walk to suit your physical condition. If you are unfit, or pregnant, or have a diagnosed medical condition which affects your ability to exercise, then check first with your doctor.

You may think: 'This is a book about stress, so why is he asking me to walk faster?' The answer is because exercise is the quickest

| Steps per minute | | | Minutes | Miles |
|---|---|---|---|---|
| 2.0 ft/stride | 2.5 ft/stride | 3.0 ft/stride | per mile | per hour |
| 90 | 70 | 60 | 30 | 2 |
| 110 | 90 | 75 | 24 | 2.5 |
| 130 | 105 | 90 | 20 | 3 |
| 155 | 120 | 105 | 17 | 3.5 |
| 175 | 140 | 120 | 15 | 4 |
| 200 | 160 | 135 | 13 | 4.5 |
| 220 | 175 | 145 | 12 | 5 |

way to give yourself a psychological boost and get some oxygen surging around your body. Brisk walking is an aerobic exercise, and the easiest way for most people to become active.

Everyone's doing it – Jane Fonda, Cher, Oprah Winfrey, even Arnie Schwarzenegger. They are all discovering that walking is the most effective exercise to keep up long-term. It's virtually injury-free and you can do it anywhere, anytime. You can do it alone, with your partner, a friend or a co-worker, or with the family.

Of course, speed isn't everything. It helps to get the oxygen flowing around the body and it's good for an energising aerobic workout, and to get those 'feel-good' hormones circulating freely. But there are times when you will want to slow down, have a stroll, meander a little, just do your own thing. That's the beauty about walking. To run or jog, you begin at a pace which for many is already too strenuous. That's why there is a high drop-out rate from such exercise, often with injuries. Walking is different – you set the pace, and you build the pace gradually to suit yourself.

# Getting Started

As you begin your 30-day plan, keep clearly in mind your goal ahead – the next 30 days and how you're going to get there. To help you with this, I have designed an interactive plan for you to refer to each day and write in your own thoughts, feelings and observations. Use it as an anti-stress 'To do' list, as follows:

- Read the topic for that day.
- Browse the 'Thoughts for the day'.
- In 'My Personal Plan', write in the positive actions you intend to take that day.
- Fill in the walking log – time planned, when and where.
- Finish the day by writing in the results of your positive actions and time walked.

The best time to plan your day is the previous evening, when you can leisurely make your arrangements. Read the next day's topic and thoughts, and decide on the positive actions you intend taking. At the end of that day, you can then reflect on the day's events and make notes about your experiences. If convenient, carry this book around with you and refer to it during the day.

Planning in this way will help you visualise the day ahead. It will keep your mind on your goals and objectives, and it will keep you motivated. There is a sense of mastery and self-reliance that comes from meeting goals that you have set. And when you know where you are going, it's so much easier to get there.

Thirty days isn't very long. Just hang in there. Anyone can keep up a 30-day walking plan – even you. And at the end of 30 days you will be motivated to follow through and maintain an enjoyable exercise that you can keep up for the rest of your life. So let's step away from stress . . .

# DAY 1: First Footing – Step This Way

You now know that walking is the perfect exercise to stress-proof your day, so let's begin day one with an early-morning energy-booster. No excuses. A 20-minute or even 10-minute walk will do you far more good than the extra time spent in bed. And it will improve your mood and energy level for the rest of the day. Remember those circadian rhythms we talked about earlier. As you sleep, your body temperature and heart rate are normally lower. Taking that early-morning walk will rev up your system. It will elevate your deep body temperature, get your circulation going and fill you full of verve and vitality for the day ahead.

So step out with a brisk, confident stride and, as the song says, 'Look the world right in the eye'. The world is your oyster; you have a right to be here. Think of your morning walk as a way of creating your own personal space – a quiet time when you can prepare for the day ahead.

**Thoughts for the day:**

- **Today is the first day of the rest of your life.**
- **Get active – set your alarm 20 minutes earlier.**
- **Health warning! Walking can seriously improve your health.**

# My Personal Plan for Day 1

## Positive Actions

_____
_____
_____
_____
_____
_____
_____

## Walking Log

| | |
|---|---|
| Time Planned | (mins) |
| Time Walked | (mins) |
| When | a.m./p.m. |
| Where | |

## Results

_____
_____
_____
_____
_____
_____
_____

# DAY 2: Walk Tall

Walk tall to feel on top of the world and to maintain a body posture which will carry you effortlessly through the day. Poor posture puts stress on your vital organs, sapping your body and energy levels. Good posture tones your body and improves oxygen flow and blood circulation.

The key to a natural walking technique is to think tall. Imagine a piece of string stretching upwards through your body and out of the top of your head towards the sky. Then imagine the string pulling you upwards like a puppet. When you walk, keep your back straight, pull in your stomach and tuck in your buttocks under your spine. Walk with your head level and eyes focused straight ahead. Keep your shoulders back, down and relaxed.

During the day, whenever you are standing, take the strain from your posture by standing with your feet apart and balancing your body weight over both legs.

**Thoughts for the day:**

- **Think tall; think perfect posture.**
- **Be loose and natural.**
- **Keep focused – develop a sense of mindful awareness.**

# My Personal Plan for Day 2

## Positive Actions

_____
_____
_____
_____
_____
_____
_____
_____

## Walking Log

Time Planned _____ (mins)
Time Walked _____ (mins)
When _____ a.m./p.m.
Where _____
_____
_____

## Results

_____
_____
_____
_____
_____
_____
_____
_____
_____

# DAY 3: Think Positive

Are you a pessimist who sees a glass as half empty or an optimist who sees a glass as half full? Optimists not only expect things to turn out well, but take positive actions to change the course of events. Optimism empowers. Optimists approach stressful events as opportunities for change and growth, and turn obstacles into stepping stones. Optimists do better in the face of stress by using coping strategies to increase their chances of success. Here's a few to optimise your day:

1. Optimists plan, so organise your day and break problems down into more manageable sizes.
2. Focus on objectives. Reflect on past emotions and past successes to keep going when others might quit.
3. Use positive self-talk to reinforce your confidence: 'I am organised and in control of my life. I have drive, determination and self-belief. I am a winner.'
4. Under stress, approach friends, family and co-workers for help and advice. Follow it.

**Thoughts for the day:**

- **Tell yourself you can.**
- **If you can't change the situation, change your attitude.**
- **Empower yourself with positive actions.**

# My Personal Plan for Day 3

## Positive Actions

_____
_____
_____
_____
_____
_____
_____
_____

## Walking Log

Time Planned _____ (mins)
Time Walked _____ (mins)
When _____ a.m./p.m.
Where _____
_____

## Results

_____
_____
_____
_____
_____
_____
_____
_____
_____

# DAY 4: Getting in the Rhythm

Today we are going to really get moving and get into the rhythm – become a swinger. To develop a natural walking rhythm, you need to continue thinking tall and give some thought to what the rest of your body is doing.

You walk tall from your heels upwards, pushing off with the ball and toes of your back foot and landing in the middle of your front heel, in a heel-toe rolling motion. Then, taking the longest stride which is comfortable, lead with your hips, and let your arms swing naturally in opposition to your legs. Keeping your elbows close to your sides, relax your shoulders and let your arms find their own rhythm.

Breathing naturally through your nose, ensure that your hands are relaxed, not clenched and tensed. As you begin to walk faster, your arms will bend naturally and the motion will be more vigorous to keep up with the action of the legs. Regular, rhythmic walking in this way will help you relax, and it has profound psychological and meditational benefits.

**Thoughts for the day:**

- **Repeat the mantra: heel–toe . . . heel–toe . . . heel–toe.**
- **Swing those arms.**
- **Deep breaths.**

# My Personal Plan for Day 4

## Positive Actions

_____
_____
_____
_____
_____
_____
_____

## Walking Log

Time Planned _____ (mins)
Time Walked _____ (mins)
When _____ a.m./p.m.
Where _____
_____

## Results

_____
_____
_____
_____
_____
_____
_____
_____

# DAY 5: Step up the Carbs

After observing the eating habits of the healthiest people across the world, many nutritionists advise that the healthiest diet contains:

- 50–60 per cent complex carbohydrates such as bread, potatoes, cereal, rice and pasta.
- At least five portions of fruit and vegetables a day.
- 20–25 per cent protein – and very little saturated fat.

These are the foods to concentrate mostly on and build your meals around. All calories are not equal. Fat contains nine calories per gram, whereas carbohydrate and protein contain only four calories per gram. And whereas the body expends only 3 per cent of every 100 calories of fat in internal processing, carbohydrate burns a healthy 27 per cent. So go for the burn and step up the carbs.

Carbohydrates are high-octane fuel. They're cheaper to buy, better for your heart and blood vessels – and they're less fattening. They are a healthy source of energy and they trigger the brain chemical serotonin, which soothes you and helps you relax.

**Thoughts for the day:**

- **You are what you eat.**
- **It's the fat in your diet that makes you fat.**
- **Eat smart – increase the carbs.**

# My Personal Plan for Day 5

## Positive Actions

---

## Walking Log

| | |
|---|---|
| Time Planned | (mins) |
| Time Walked | (mins) |
| When | a.m./p.m. |
| Where | |

## Results

---

# DAY 6: Give Yourself an Oxygen Boost

Energise your walks by walking faster. Get into a comfortable rhythm, then gradually increase your speed. Use the steps/minute chart on page 36 to gauge speed. Don't push yourself too hard – if you can't hold a conversation without getting out of breath, you are walking too fast. Walk aerobics is the quickest way to get oxygen surging through your body and it gives you an instant stress–busting lift.

Warm up by walking for three or four minutes at normal pace before increasing speed, and cool down at the end by reducing speed over a few minutes. This will ensure you stay clear of pulled muscles and other injuries. And remember to fill in your walking log. It is a way of praising and rewarding yourself, and it builds up a record of achievement which you can look back on later. You need all the help you can get when you are trying to build long-term habits. Give yourself an oxygen boost whenever you feel tired, tense or anxious.

**Thoughts for the day:**

- **Oxygen is free! So don't be afraid to use it.**
- **Burning more oxygen burns more body fat.**
- **Take a breather any time your mind is flagging.**

# My Personal Plan for Day 6

## Positive Actions

_____
_____
_____
_____
_____
_____
_____
_____

## Walking Log

| | |
|---|---|
| Time Planned | (mins) |
| Time Walked | (mins) |
| When | a.m./p.m. |
| Where | |

## Results

_____
_____
_____
_____
_____
_____
_____
_____

# DAY 7: Laugh and Smile

The economist John Maynard Keynes brings us all down to earth when he reminds us: 'In the long run, we are all dead.' What then of the 'getting and spending', 'the profit and the loss'? The Chinese writer and philosopher Lin Yutang said: 'The world is far too serious, and being far too serious, it has need of a wise and merry philosophy.' Yutang believed in simple living and he wanted people to become 'laughing philosophers', feeling first life's tragedy and then life's comedy.

So smile today and reflect on your own mortality. A smile ignites a positive mood. And find the time to bring some laughter into your own and others' lives – a sense of humour is one of the best ways to fend off stress. Laughter is the shortest distance between people. Stress-fighting brain chemicals are released when we laugh. And laughing is like internal aerobics – it deepens breathing, increases circulation and relaxes our muscles.

As the Chinese say: 'The most wasted day is that in which we have not laughed.'

**Thoughts for the day:**

- **Laughter is the best medicine.**
- **Smile more – the world will be a happier place.**
- **Take life more slowly – be more philosophical.**

# My Personal Plan for Day 7

## Positive Actions

---
---
---
---
---
---
---

## Walking Log

Time Planned ............................................. (mins)
Time Walked ............................................. (mins)
When ............................................. a.m./p.m.
Where .............................................

## Results

---
---
---
---
---
---
---
---

# DAY 8: Plan for Stress

No one can escape from stress. Even battle-hardened executives can suffer a fit of madness if they have to make a speech. Market research shows that the number-one fear for most people is the fear of speaking before a group. But if it's a speech you have to make, or you simply have to juggle time to fit everything into your day, planning for a stressful situation is half the battle.

Don't adopt a fire-fighting attitude to stress, reacting to problems as they arise. Anticipate stressful situations. Remember the motto 'Know thyself'? Use your self-knowledge of how you feel in tense situations in order to plan the most effective way to deal with them. Then, if you feel stressed, do a 60-second stress scan. Stop, take a deep breath and check in with your body. The rhythmic action of breathing is soothing and helps you focus and centre yourself. Continue breathing deeply, and you will find yourself relaxing naturally. Or take a stretch break, or give yourself an oxygen boost with a power walk.

**Thoughts for the day:**

- **Plan ahead – be prepared.**
- **In a tense situation, take a deep breath and refocus.**
- **Take regular stretch breaks.**

# My Personal Plan for Day 8

## Positive Actions

_____

_____

_____

_____

_____

_____

_____

## Walking Log

Time Planned _____ (mins)
Time Walked _____ (mins)
When _____ a.m./p.m.
Where _____

_____

## Results

_____

_____

_____

_____

_____

_____

_____

_____

# DAY 9: On the Road

Commuter traffic and traffic jams are a major source of stress or 'road rage', so add extra time to journeys to compensate. Remember that you're not Michael Schumacher or Jacques Villeneuve. Don't contest every driver in his 'ego chariot' who tries to move into your lane. Let them cut in. Let them take all the stress. Just sit back and let the journey take the strain.

Stress diminishes the output of the heart. When drivers get angry, they produce the 'fight or flight' hormone adrenaline, which narrows the arteries. Dr Ian Baird of the British Heart Foundation says: 'Some people also overbreathe, or hyperventilate, which can have the same effect.'

Driving fast requires more alertness, more readiness to respond and more muscle tension. So plan your journey, allowing time for delays – and slow down. If you get stuck in a jam, use your time constructively: relax to some music, or plan a weekend away. You'll feel less stressed and more tolerant at the end of your journey.

**Thoughts for the day:**

- **Relax – let everyone else blow off steam.**
- **Use the time to visualise the day ahead.**
- **Listen to audio cassettes – learn a language.**

# My Personal Plan for Day 9

## Positive Actions

_____
_____
_____
_____
_____
_____
_____

## Walking Log

Time Planned                                    (mins)
Time Walked                                     (mins)
When                                         a.m./p.m.
Where _____
_____

## Results

_____
_____
_____
_____
_____
_____
_____
_____

# DAY 10: Junk the Caffeine

Need a break or feel stressed? What do most people reach for? A caffeine fix. Yet caffeine and other stimulants in coffee, tea and cola drinks boost the output of stress hormones and cause the body to work overtime. They make you more alert and give you a buzz, but it's not long before you need another fix. Caffeine in these drinks takes six hours to work its way through your system, and too much can cause sleep loss. And don't think that decaff is the answer – you're then stuck with harmful additives used in its manufacture.

Junk the caffeine and try herbal teas or, better still, a water workout. Water is the most important nutrient required by the body and is needed by all the body's processes. Carry a bottle of water around with you and drink often. When you are under stress you sweat more and your mouth tends to dry up. You'll feel better if you hydrate your anxiety and tensions away with water. Begin your day with a detox – a squeeze of fresh lemon juice in water.

**Thoughts for the day:**

- **Caffeine may boost your mood but it also boosts stress.**
- **Junk the coffee break – take a walk.**
- **Water – best drink of the day (drink at least six glasses).**

# My Personal Plan for Day 10

## Positive Actions

_____
_____
_____
_____
_____
_____
_____

## Walking Log

Time Planned _____ (mins)
Time Walked _____ (mins)
When _____ a.m./p.m.
Where _____
_____

## Results

_____
_____
_____
_____
_____
_____
_____
_____

# DAY 11: Be More Assertive

If you are going to survive stressful situations you need a positive attitude about yourself – you need to be assertive. When you are assertive, you make a positive statement about who you are; you tell others confidently what you want or what you need. And your body language is confident: you stand well-balanced on both feet and look directly at the person you are speaking to, using a calm, level tone of voice. Assertive speakers begin with positive words like 'I', 'I think', 'I would like', and they use co-operative phrases such as 'We could' or 'Shall we?'.

Being assertive doesn't mean being aggressive. Aggressive, confrontational behaviour alienates others and ignites stressful situations; assertive behaviour increases self-esteem and self-confidence, and promotes a co-operative and friendly environment.

One way of raising your self-esteem is to remind yourself what you're good at and what you do well. Define your 'magnificence'. Write down a list of all your positive characteristics. It's the best way to feel good about yourself and your achievements.

**Thoughts for the day:**

- **Don't internalise emotions – communicate them.**
- **Express your feelings – ask for what you need.**
- **Remind yourself regularly of your positive strengths – write them down.**

# My Personal Plan for Day 11

## Positive Actions

_____
_____
_____
_____
_____
_____
_____
_____

## Walking Log

Time Planned _____ (mins)
Time Walked _____ (mins)
When _____ a.m./p.m.
Where _____
_____
_____

## Results

_____
_____
_____
_____
_____
_____
_____
_____
_____

# DAY 12: Footnotes

The feet carry the entire weight of the body, holding it upright and maintaining its balance and rhythm during walking. Acting as shock-absorbers, they soak up the stresses and strains which harass our bodies throughout the day. So to ensure your walking is stress-free, it's important to protect your feet.

Always make sure you buy shoes which are comfortable, not just fashionable. These days you can buy specialist walking shoes designed for the beach and the boardroom. Buy shoes late in the day, as the feet tend to swell as the day wears on. Ensure that there's enough room in the toe-box to wiggle your toes, and never suffer sales talk about shoes stretching and wearing in – they rarely do. If a shoe isn't comfortable, don't buy it.

At the end of the day, try pampering your feet with a long soak in the bath, adding an aromatherapy oil. Or splash out and buy yourself a foot spa. If you look after your feet, they'll look after you.

**Thoughts for the day:**

- **Feet first – those feet were made for walking.**
- **Don't accept discomfort – wear cushioned, roomy shoes.**
- **Consider socks – cushioned if possible. Change daily.**

# My Personal Plan for Day 12

## Positive Actions

_____
_____
_____
_____
_____
_____
_____

## Walking Log

| | |
|---|---|
| Time Planned | (mins) |
| Time Walked | (mins) |
| When | a.m./p.m. |
| Where | |

## Results

_____
_____
_____
_____
_____
_____
_____
_____
_____

# DAY 13: The Food of Love

Healthy eating is important, but it's also important to let your hair down once in a while. Follow the 80/20 rule. If you eat healthily for at least 80 per cent of the time, it probably won't matter too much if you vary your diet for the remaining 20 per cent. Healthy eating, of course, shouldn't mean having to endure unexciting, bland food. Follow *The Rhythm for Life*'s anti-stress diet for maximum health and enjoyment.

At weekends there is more time to prepare foods in a mindful, loving way. Cooking itself can be a type of meditation. Let food be the music of love. Prepare fresh, organic foods rather than processed, convenience foods. Experiment with different cuisines, different tastes and different combinations of foods. And what better way to relax than to enjoy a meal with friends, family or an intimate dinner with your partner? Establish rhythm and harmony in your life with good food and good company, and enrich your evening by playing some inspiring music to help you soothe away the stresses and strains of the past week.

**Thoughts for the day:**

- **Cut out processed, convenience foods – think fresh, organic, healthy foods.**
- **Make a point of organising that special evening with friends or loved ones.**
- **Take a stroll after dinner – it will help you relax and release muscular tension.**

# My Personal Plan for Day 13

## Positive Actions

_____
_____
_____
_____
_____
_____
_____
_____

## Walking Log

Time Planned _____ (mins)
Time Walked _____ (mins)
When _____ a.m./p.m.
Where _____
_____

## Results

_____
_____
_____
_____
_____
_____
_____
_____

# DAY 14: Focusing in on your Time

Under pressure you can lose sight of priorities, allowing certain activities to crowd out others and leaving you harassed, stressed and unable to cope. By organising your time efficiently, you will feel you are in control of your life. Here are four winning ways to destress your time:

1. Make a personal inventory of how you spend your time by keeping a diary for a fortnight and writing down in 15- or 30-minute increments what you have done. It can be very revealing. Eliminate unproductive time-stealers.

2. Spend time thinking about your goals – major and minor; short-, intermediate- and long-term. Then allocate time to specific tasks to accomplish them.

3. Learn to prioritise. Make a daily 'To do' list and divide tasks into three categories: urgent and important; important; not urgent and not important. Plan and review as you begin and end each day.

4. Set specific, realistic deadlines to pre-empt frustration, panic and crises. Allow time for distractions, interruptions and emergencies.

**Thoughts for the day:**

- **Plan ahead and focus in on your goals.**
- **Prioritise and assign time to 'important' tasks.**
- **Be proactive – not reactive.**

# My Personal Plan for Day 14

## Positive Actions

_____
_____
_____
_____
_____
_____
_____
_____

## Walking Log

Time Planned                                    (mins)
Time Walked                                      (mins)
When                                        a.m./p.m.
Where
_____
_____

## Results

_____
_____
_____
_____
_____
_____
_____
_____

# DAY 15: Try Music Therapy

Music has been used as therapy since David played his harp for troubled King Saul. The right music can take you from a highly tense state to a relaxed, alert state in a matter of minutes. So slip on your headphones and start walking. Within minutes you begin to move into a flow state, opening up your mind, body and spirit to new possibilities and potentials. Feel the euphoric rush of energy release as you move into a measured step with the rhythm of the music, and experience an instant 'high'. After 30 minutes, your body has had an aerobic workout, your muscles are stretched and toned and you feel on top of the world.

Instrumental pieces on piano, flute, harp or string ensembles tend to be more soothing than vocal pieces. Experiment with music at different tempos to match your walking rhythm, whether a stroll or a brisk workout. Just a note of caution: headphones can distract you from traffic and other dangers on the road, so be careful when and where you use them.

**Thoughts for the day:**

- **Add excitement and energy to your walking workout.**
- **Play tunes that move – match the tempo to your stride and mood.**
- **It can take as little as 30 seconds to begin walking away from a highly tense state.**

# My Personal Plan for Day 15

## Positive Actions

_____
_____
_____
_____
_____
_____
_____

## Walking Log

Time Planned                                    (mins)
Time Walked                                      (mins)
When                                          a.m./p.m.
Where
_____

## Results

_____
_____
_____
_____
_____
_____
_____
_____

# DAY 16: Raw Energy

Stress and poor nutrition can lead to a slowing-down of metabolic processes due to an accumulation of wastes and toxins. Counteract this and give yourself a mind lift by starting the day with raw energy – uncooked foods such as fruits, vegetables, nuts, grains, seeds and sprouts. A raw diet will help you lose weight and feel fitter and younger, and it will give you the vitality and resistance to withstand stress and tiredness.

Crudités (raw vegetables cut into bite-sized pieces) provide a nutritious and delicious starter, or are in themselves a healthy snack. Cut the vegetables as close in time to eating them as possible, otherwise valuable nutrients may be lost. Try a selection from the following: carrots, celery, green and red peppers, cauliflower florets, radishes, cucumber.

Fruit is the most available form of raw energy. And there's more to fruit than apples, oranges and bananas – try some of the many exciting fruits readily available: mango, papaya, figs, kiwi fruit, pineapple, melons, passion fruit. Raw foods are a quick and easy way to get a high-energy lift.

**Thoughts for the day:**

- **Detox your body for natural health and vitality.**
- **A raw diet will allow you to work harder – and your thought processes will be clearer.**
- **Snack on raw foods at any time of the day for an energy boost.**

# My Personal Plan for Day 16

## Positive Actions

_____
_____
_____
_____
_____
_____
_____

## Walking Log

Time Planned _____ (mins)
Time Walked _____ (mins)
When _____ a.m./p.m.
Where _____
_____
_____

## Results

_____
_____
_____
_____
_____
_____
_____
_____

# DAY 17: Desk Stress – Reducing the Strain

A sedentary lifestyle poses the greatest single risk to the collective health of us all. Sitting over a desk automatically increases muscle tension in the neck, shoulders and upper arms. So next time you're stuck for long periods at a desk or in front of a computer, try these quick methods to relax and ease the build-up of tension:

1. Take microbreaks while using the computer. Every ten minutes remove your hands from the keyboard and relax the fingers. Look away from the screen to reduce eye strain.
2. Take a stretch break every 30 minutes to relax muscles. Get up and walk around; do a few simple stretches (see Nine to Five stretches in chapter three). Move your printer across the room to force you to get out of the chair.
3. Take six deep breaths – this is enough to instantly reduce blood pressure and make you feel calmer.
4. Take a ten-minute walking break and also walk in the lunch hour. Extensive research carried out at California State University in the USA confirms significant stress-reduction benefits.

**Thoughts for the day:**

- **Take a lot of mini-breaks to calm and relax, and reduce arm, shoulder and neck strain.**
- **If you feel tension starting to grip – centre yourself, focus and breathe deeply.**
- **Don't let desk stress pull you down – get up, move around and stretch.**

# My Personal Plan for Day 17

## Positive Actions

_____

_____

_____

_____

_____

_____

_____

_____

## Walking Log

Time Planned _____ (mins)
Time Walked _____ (mins)
When _____ a.m./p.m.
Where _____

_____

## Results

_____

_____

_____

_____

_____

_____

_____

_____

# DAY 18: Let off Steam

People who bottle up destructive emotions suffer more from stress than those who get it out in the open. Unresolved anger eats you up from the inside and increases adrenaline, which in turn increases blood pressure. Periods of stress create self-doubt, and, unresolved, these emotions can run away with themselves.

Sartre was right: at times hell really can be other people – people who ride rough-shod over other people's feelings and emotions without any sense of shame. Don't be pushed around. Stand up to them. Learn to say no. Remember that the bully is often a coward and backs away from confrontation. Be assertive. State your own position quietly and firmly and others will respect you for it.

Another way to let off steam is to put a bunch of fresh herbs – rosemary, parsley, marjoram and basil – into a bowl of boiling water. Lean over and put a towel over your head and around the bowl. The steam will open up the skin's pores, oxygenate and cleanse the cells and increase circulation. And you will feel your cares and troubles just melt away.

**Thoughts for the day:**

- **Don't bottle it up – talk it out.**
- **Be more assertive – don't give in to bullies.**
- **Steam away your cares with hydrotherapy.**

# My Personal Plan for Day 18

## Positive Actions

_____
_____
_____
_____
_____
_____
_____

## Walking Log

| | |
|---|---:|
| Time Planned | (mins) |
| Time Walked | (mins) |
| When | a.m./p.m. |
| Where | |

_____
_____

## Results

_____
_____
_____
_____
_____
_____
_____
_____

# DAY 19: Go for the Burn

If you want to lose weight and whittle away those unwanted pounds, try walking faster.

Depending on your weight, you can burn 350 to 400 calories an hour at 4 mph. But for most people 3.5 mph is a good fat-burning speed, and it's much easier to keep up day in, day out. When you begin to walk faster, don't push yourself too hard. If you find it's difficult, ease back to a comfortable speed – you may burn more calories by walking longer rather than harder.

Increase cardiovascular fitness and burn more calories by walking up hills or on uneven ground. You will burn 50 per cent more calories walking at 4 mph on a 5 per cent gradient, and 100 per cent more calories on a 10 per cent gradient. After meals, try a gentle stroll. It will help digestion, increase your energy and burn extra calories. And eat more complex carbohydrates such as bread, cereal, rice and pasta. It's exercise and healthy eating that will guarantee a successful burn.

**Thoughts for the day:**

- **A brisk walk burns fat and burns away stress.**
- **Walk up stairs and avoid lifts and escalators.**
- **Eat more carbs to fuel your metabolic furnace.**

# My Personal Plan for Day 19

## Positive Actions

_____
_____
_____
_____
_____
_____
_____
_____

## Walking Log

Time Planned _____ (mins)
Time Walked _____ (mins)
When _____ a.m./p.m.
Where _____
_____
_____

## Results

_____
_____
_____
_____
_____
_____
_____
_____
_____

# DAY 20: Take Pleasure in Nature

*'I went to the woods because I wished to live deliberately, to front only the essential facts of life, and see if I could not learn what it had to teach.'*

These are the words of the American writer Thoreau. Like Thoreau, we can learn from nature. Nature entices us to return to our roots and live a simpler, more peaceful life. A walk in the woods, or by the river or seaside, is a way of getting away from it all and restoring our mental and physical batteries. Look upon your outing as a journey. Journeys, like holidays, can be magical. They are a time to regenerate, let go and relax. To walk and talk, and stand and stare. They are a way of getting in touch with reality. 'When we're overloaded with everyday concerns, nature takes us away from our problems,' says David C. Glass, PhD, a professor of psychology at State University of New York. 'The break allows us to restore our energy. It could have tremendous benefits in alleviating negative feelings.'

**Thoughts for the day:**

- **Create more space to stand and stare.**
- **Let nature work its magic on you.**
- **Try 'roamertherapy' – surprise yourself with an impromptu outing.**

# My Personal Plan for Day 20

## Positive Actions

_____
_____
_____
_____
_____
_____
_____
_____

## Walking Log

Time Planned _____ (mins)
Time Walked _____ (mins)
When _____ a.m./p.m.
Where _____
_____

## Results

_____
_____
_____
_____
_____
_____
_____
_____
_____

# DAY 21: Talk away your Troubles

Go for a walk with a friend and talk away your troubles. They say that a friend is the best psychiatrist. Walking in the fresh air provides food for the spirit, and it helps you talk problems through and get to the root of what's bothering you.

Try different venues. Walk in the woods – and feel a special intimacy with the trees, the leaves, the rocks and the smells all around you. Walk by the sea – the sea's ebb and flow pulses like the rhythm of your own heartbeat and the alternating motion of your arms and legs. The healing power of rhythm can free destructive emotions and can help you relax and let go. Research shows that a 20–30-minute brisk walk can have the same effect as a mild tranquilliser, and it can reduce depression and enhance self-esteem.

Take your partner, a work colleague or even the kids on your walk – and talk. Or simply walk alone and use positive self-talk to clear up your troubles.

**Thoughts for the day:**

- **Got a problem? Walk it off.**
- **Take a friend, partner – or the family.**
- **'Walktalk' is the best therapy there is.**

# My Personal Plan for Day 21

## Positive Actions

_____
_____
_____
_____
_____
_____
_____

## Walking Log

Time Planned _____ (mins)
Time Walked _____ (mins)
When _____ a.m./p.m.
Where _____
_____

## Results

_____
_____
_____
_____
_____
_____
_____
_____

# DAY 22: Put your Heart into It

The British Heart Foundation shocked the nation when it announced that lack of exercise can be as bad for us as smoking 20 cigarettes a day, or having high cholesterol or high blood pressure. Studies in several countries have found that the least active people are twice as likely to have heart disease as the most active. And the exercise most recommended by all these studies? Walking briskly for at least 20 minutes three or four times a week is the easiest and safest way to become active and protect your heart.

The Paffenburger study in the USA found that walking two miles a day can lower your chance of a heart attack by up to 30 per cent. The Health Education Authority in Britain says: 'Regular activity of this kind improves the balance of fatty substances in the bloodstream, lowers the resting blood pressure and strengthens the heart muscle.' So keep your heart in good shape and walk for at least 20 minutes today, knowing you can look forward to a longer, fitter and healthier life.

**Thoughts for the day:**

- **Focus – what is the heart of the matter? Walking.**
- **Be more active – walk more often.**
- **Visualise a long, happy, healthy life.**

# My Personal Plan for Day 22

## Positive Actions

_____
_____
_____
_____
_____
_____
_____
_____

## Walking Log

Time Planned _____ (mins)
Time Walked _____ (mins)
When _____ a.m./p.m.
Where _____
_____

## Results

_____
_____
_____
_____
_____
_____
_____
_____

# DAY 23: Vital Vitamins

Vitamins A, C and E, known as antioxidants, help to fight off the effects of stress and ageing caused by free radicals released from adrenaline, the stress hormone. Free radicals are produced as part of normal body chemistry and they can attack blood vessels and vital organs, causing irreversible cell damage. Eating foods rich in vitamins A (beta-carotene), C and E will help protect against the destructive reactions caused by free radicals. They are found in the following:

**Beta-carotene**: dark leafy vegetables, yellow and orange vegetables and fruits such as broccoli, spinach, peas, cress, asparagus, carrots, sweet potatoes, tomatoes, apricots, peaches, cherries, mangoes, cantaloup melon.

**Vitamin C**: citrus fruit, kiwi fruit, strawberries, blackcurrants, raw cabbage, green leafy vegetables, green peppers, potatoes, parsnips, swedes, tomatoes.

**Vitamin E**: whole grains, nuts, seeds, soya beans, vegetable oils especially sunflower oil, fish liver oils, green leafy vegetables.

**Thoughts for the day:**

- **Boost intake of antioxidant vitamins.**
- **ACE eating: look younger, live longer, feel healthier.**
- **Protect yourself from disease.**

# My Personal Plan for Day 23

## Positive Actions

_____

_____

_____

_____

_____

_____

_____

## Walking Log

Time Planned _____ (mins)
Time Walked _____ (mins)
When _____ a.m./p.m.
Where _____

_____

## Results

_____

_____

_____

_____

_____

_____

_____

_____

# DAY 24: Watch your Back

Four out of five people suffer from back pain at some time in their lives. A sedentary lifestyle – too much time spent sitting and not enough exercising – and poor posture can cause back problems and weak back muscles. So sit up straight. Good posture improves breathing and increases blood flow to the brain. We often slouch when stressed; this restricts breathing and blood flow, and it can magnify our feelings of helplessness.

To watch your back, maintain good posture, breathe normally, shift your position at least every 20 minutes, stretch regularly and take frequent exercise breaks. Dr John Regan, a surgeon at the Texas Back Institute, makes this recommendation: 'Taking a walk regularly is one of the best things you can do for your back. It promotes muscular development and increases circulation.' Walking helps strengthen and tone your back muscles, and the natural rhythmic action of walking promotes good posture and helps reduce muscle tension – two key factors in maintaining a healthy back.

**Thoughts for the day:**

- **Treat your own back. Think positive – sit up straight.**
- **Back to basics – go for a walk.**
- **Regular walking will exercise back muscles, reduce tension and increase circulation.**

# My Personal Plan for Day 24

## Positive Actions

_____
_____
_____
_____
_____
_____
_____
_____

## Walking Log

Time Planned _____ (mins)
Time Walked _____ (mins)
When _____ a.m./p.m.
Where _____
_____

## Results

_____
_____
_____
_____
_____
_____
_____
_____

# DAY 25: Walk, Weather or Not

Don't be put off by the weather. Follow the changing face of the seasons and dress suitably. On cold days, keep your extremities warm – cover your head and neck, wear gloves and keep your thighs well covered. Wear light layers of clothing that you can add to or remove while you walk. In warm weather, wear light-coloured clothes to reflect heat and light and a broad-brimmed hat in bright sunshine.

Don't let the weather get you down. If you feel those sad, winter blues coming on, walk into the light. On the greyest day there is often a break in the light. It may be early morning, around noon, or in the evening. Follow the light like a painter does. Walk through the shifting patterns of light and expand your mind to take in your surroundings. Follow your own inner light – get out of your mind, out of yourself, and out of the vicious circle of negative thoughts depressing you. Ask a friend to accompany you and try some 'walktalk'; it's the best therapy there is.

**Thoughts for the day:**

- **View the weather as an opportunity – not a threat.**
- **Don't let Seasonal Affective Disorder (SAD) get you down. Walk into the light.**
- **Study the subtle nuances and shades of the changing light.**

# My Personal Plan for Day 25

## Positive Actions

_____
_____
_____
_____
_____
_____
_____

## Walking Log

Time Planned _____ (mins)
Time Walked _____ (mins)
When _____ a.m./p.m.
Where _____
_____

## Results

_____
_____
_____
_____
_____
_____
_____
_____

# DAY 26: Helping Others

At times we become absorbed by our own problems and think that life is giving us a raw deal. Remind yourself today that your problems may not amount to very much compared with those of a starving refugee or someone who is terminally ill. Consider giving some time to others. Get involved in a voluntary activity you genuinely support. A ten-year study at the University of Michigan found that the death rate was twice as high in men who did no volunteer work as in men who volunteered their time at least once a week.

Helping others not only helps them, but it will also help take you out of yourself and put your life into perspective. And it will give you a sense of accomplishment and self-respect. No man, or woman, is an island. None of us can be truly aloof and independent. We all live in an interdependent community where we rely on others for friendship, co-operation and help. So today think of others less fortunate than yourself, and consider offering a helping hand.

**Thoughts for the day:**

- **Think more of others.**
- **Reflect on ways you can offer help – time, money, expertise.**
- **'No man is an island' – John Donne.**

# My Personal Plan for Day 26

## Positive Actions

_____
_____
_____
_____
_____
_____
_____

## Walking Log

Time Planned _____ (mins)
Time Walked _____ (mins)
When _____ a.m./p.m.
Where _____
_____
_____

## Results

_____
_____
_____
_____
_____
_____
_____
_____

# DAY 27: Meditation and Mindfulness

Meditation allows the mind to settle into a state of deep calm and relaxation – like turning down the volume on a radio. Meditation works because you focus on only one thing at a time. Find a quiet place to sit comfortably for 20 minutes without being disturbed. Close your eyes and begin repeating silently to yourself 'one . . . one . . . one'. Don't worry about how well you are doing. If your mind wanders and thoughts enter, accept their presence, let them go, and bring your mind back to repeating 'one . . . one . . . one'.

For a change, try walking meditation. The idea is to cultivate mindfulness and awareness. The world at 3.5 mph looks a far different place from the world seen from a car or train. Savour the sights and sounds of your walks and open your eyes to the world around you. Walking meditation can give you a feeling of joy, balance and peace; it is the perfect way to spend part of your lunch hour or some time before or after work, or a relaxing way to get out over the weekend.

**Thoughts for the day:**

- **A healthy mind in a healthy body.**
- **Turn off to tune in – meditate for 20 minutes.**
- **Try walking meditation.**

# My Personal Plan for Day 27

## Positive Actions

_____
_____
_____
_____
_____
_____
_____
_____

## Walking Log

Time Planned _____ (mins)
Time Walked _____ (mins)
When _____ a.m./p.m.
Where _____
_____

## Results

_____
_____
_____
_____
_____
_____
_____
_____
_____

# DAY 28: Visualisation

Most of us visualise all the time, but often in the wrong frame of mind. A negative frame of mind produces negative results; a positive frame of mind produces positive results. Someone going on holiday who is worrying about the weather is already thinking negatively, whereas someone with a positive attitude will probably make the most of the holiday despite the weather.

Scientists tell us that normally we use as little as 10 per cent of our mind's potential. The technique of visualisation allows us to tap into some of that unused potential and focus on specific goals. Visualisation is getting the mind to see yourself doing what you want to do. Sportsmen use visualisation to 'see' their desired goal, whether it's hitting a ball or winning a race. It's the same with exercise and stress. Each morning visualise yourself walking out, getting fit and positively coping with anything the day throws at you. Your positive attitude will help you achieve your goal.

**Thoughts for the day:**

- **Set the scene – try mental rehearsal.**
- **Visualise yourself striding confidently through the day.**
- **Visualise your goals and activities with strong self-belief.**

# My Personal Plan for Day 28

## Positive Actions

_____
_____
_____
_____
_____
_____
_____
_____

## Walking Log

Time Planned _____ (mins)
Time Walked _____ (mins)
When _____ a.m./p.m.
Where _____
_____

## Results

_____
_____
_____
_____
_____
_____
_____
_____

# DAY 29: How Do You Spell Relief? W-A-L-K

Walking can be a whole philosophy of life. After all, from the moment we rise in the morning until we climb into bed at night, we are on and off our feet. So today, give some thought to the ways you can make walking part of your day. Here are six ways to give you an energy boost whenever you're flagging:

1. Kick-start your day with a brisk morning walk. If possible, walk to work.
2. Leave your bus or train one or two stops early, or leave your car a distance from your destination, and walk the rest of the way.
3. Take a walk instead of a coffee break – it will give you a better 'lift'.
4. Use stairs instead of elevators. They will tone your legs and exercise your heart.
5. Organise a lunch-time walking group with friends or work colleagues.
6. Relax and unwind with an after-dinner stroll.

**Thoughts for the day:**

- **Fit people handle stress better.**
- **Think of all the ways you can walk away from stress.**
- **Don't be a workaholic – be a walkaholic.**

# My Personal Plan for Day 29

## Positive Actions

_____

_____

_____

_____

_____

_____

_____

## Walking Log

Time Planned _____ (mins)

Time Walked _____ (mins)

When _____ a.m./p.m.

Where _____

_____

## Results

_____

_____

_____

_____

_____

_____

_____

# DAY 30: Make Tracks to Success

In recent years there has been a renaissance in walking. Suddenly, people everywhere are walking – for fun, fitness, weight loss, stress release, and as a healthy way to spend quality time with friends and family. Conventional wisdom had us pounding the pavements running and jogging, or going for the burn in high-impact workouts in the gym. Now that's all changed. Walking – fitness walking – is the smart way to get active and stay active for the rest of our lives. We were born to walk. Our anatomy has evolved to support it – firm stable foot, broad pelvis and generous buttocks.

Now, as you come to the end of your 30-day plan, you should be fitter, more active and more confident than when you started, and you should have the motivation to maintain this positive lifestyle. You will have taken active steps to let go and relax more, and you will be able to use stress in a more positive way to enrich rather than enslave you. Keep walking and you will never look back.

**Thoughts for the day:**

- **I feel more relaxed, vital, energetic and motivated.**
- **I will keep this up for the rest of my life.**
- **Walking works wonders!**

# My Personal Plan for Day 30

## Positive Actions

_____
_____
_____
_____
_____
_____
_____
_____

## Walking Log

Time Planned _____ (mins)
Time Walked _____ (mins)
When _____ a.m./p.m.
Where _____
_____

## Results

_____
_____
_____
_____
_____
_____
_____
_____

# The Third Way – Tone, Stretch and Relax

*Run your fingers along my spine
and I will purr like a cat.*
FROM A CHINESE POEM

What does a cat do after it has been asleep? It stretches. What do you do when you are tired? You yawn. Your face relaxes and you feel a sense of release. In the same way, when your whole body is supple and relaxed, you feel better physically and mentally, and you are better able to cope with the stresses and strains of modern life.

As we grow older we gradually lose the effortless grace and energy we had in our youth. Our modern sedentary lifestyle inhibits our range of natural movement. Hours spent behind the wheel of a car, sitting behind a desk or watching television rob us of the natural suppleness and flexibility we enjoyed as children. We move less and exercise less, and labour-saving devices do the work that we used to do ourselves. We are often tense and anxious, and excess tension stored in muscle tissues can become chronic if we don't release it. In the end, like any machine, our body will break down if it is neglected. But with a little effort, we can reverse the damage due to tension and inactivity, and unlock the potential in our bodies to regain our lost flexibility.

As we get older, muscles lose their elasticity and they harden when tensed. Stretching makes them looser and more elastic. Although some tension is released with sleep, it is only when muscles are stretched regularly that they become supple and release excess pent-up tension.

If you have been inactive for some time and are stiff and unfit, then approach the exercises carefully. And if you suffer from any problem that may prevent you from performing any of the movements, consult your doctor before attempting them.

Stretch whenever you feel tense, and get a boost of energy from the oxygen that is pulled deep into your lungs. Let your movements flow naturally – don't overstretch and don't force the movements. Always keep within your own ability and listen to what your body is telling you. Slowly stretch into each position, going only as far as is comfortable, hold for the required time, then come out of it slowly.

Aim to keep your breathing deep and natural throughout. As you focus on each movement, be aware of the beneficial effects of the exercise. And visualise the benefits: see the muscles loosening, stretching and becoming supple and strong. The destressing benefits of stretching will unlock your potential for boundless vitality and radiance.

# Shape up for Life

The following routines are designed to tone, stretch and relax you. They are all based on easy rhythmic movements to stimulate the circulation and ease the muscles into activity.

## Every Day

### CHECK POSTURE

Bad posture can cause injuries, back pain and muscle tension. The result? You feel sluggish, stressed and low in self-esteem. Bad posture cramps the muscles, imposing a strain on the joints and impairing the proper functioning of the internal organs. And it can prevent you from breathing properly. Correct posture and correct breathing go together. So check your posture before beginning all exercises and when walking, standing and sitting.

Apply the Alexander Technique formula (F. Matthias Alexander developed a natural and simple approach to posture and body movement that promotes flexibility and body awareness):

- Let the neck be relaxed and free; avoid increasing muscle tension in the neck.
- Let the head go forward and up, never back and down to sit on and crush the spine.
- Let the torso lengthen and widen out; avoid arching the spine.

Think tall at all times, whether sitting, standing or walking. Imagine a thread running up through your body and out of the crown of your head, pulling you upwards like a puppet. Breathe deeply and rhythmically to help you relax, and change your position regularly. After sitting for some time, walk around the room for a few minutes, concentrating on your posture, or go for a short walk. Walking is one of the best exercises for posture because it strengthens the major muscle groups that support the back, including the abdominal muscles, and the muscles on either side of the spine, buttocks and thighs.

# WARM-UPS — STRETCHES TO GET THOSE BODY RHYTHMS MOVING

*Shoulder shrugs*
To loosen and relax the neck, shoulders and upper back.

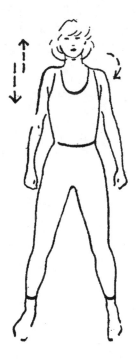

Stand tall with feet hip width apart, knees slightly bent, abdominals pulled in and pelvis tucked under. Relax arms by your sides. Lift and lower shoulders 8 times, rotate shoulders back 8 times and rotate forward 8 times.

*Upward stretch*
To loosen shoulders and chest.

Stand as above, feet slightly wider than hip width apart. Inhale as you raise arms above head, exhale as you lower arms. Repeat 4 times.

*Knee lifts*
To increase blood flow and oxygen uptake to working muscles, warming up calves, Achilles tendons and quadriceps.

Walk on the spot. Stay tall with abdominals in and a long back. Gradually increase intensity by marching and swinging arms back and forth. Alternatively, lift knees up level with your hips so that your thighs are parallel to the floor. Repeat 16 times.

*Thigh stretch*

To stretch out quadriceps, situated down the front of the thigh.

Using a chair or the wall for balance, stand on left leg with knee slightly bent, pelvis tucked under, trunk upright. Hold on to right foot, keep knees together and ease right heel towards right buttock as the right hip extends gently forwards. Hold for 10–15 seconds. Repeat with other leg.

## Hamstring curl

To increase circulation and activate and limber hamstring muscles, situated on the back of the thigh.

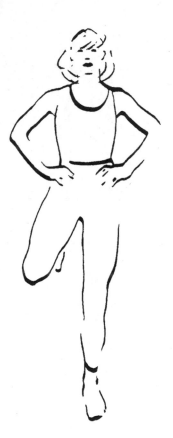

Stand with feet fairly wide apart, toes turned slightly outward, abdominals in, chest up, hands on hips. Lift right heel up and back towards right buttock, then lower foot back to floor. Repeat with left foot. Alternate these heel lifts, breathing deeply and steadily. Repeat 16 times.

*Hamstring stretch*
To pre-lengthen and prepare muscles behind thigh.

Bend left leg, hands on left thigh. Straighten out right leg in front of you. Point toes, keep knees in line. With a long trunk lean forward, slightly lifting chest and holding abdominals in (do not bend from waist). Feel the stretch behind the right thigh in the hamstring muscles as the right leg is lengthened slowly. Hold for 10–15 seconds. Repeat on other leg.

*Calf raises*
To warm and prepare calf muscles and Achilles tendon.

Stand tall, abdominals in, shoulders back and relaxed, feet together, using a wall or chair for balance. Lift heels, standing on balls of feet, and 'squeeze' into calf muscles. Hold for 2 counts, then lower heels down to floor. Repeat 6 times.

*Calf stretch*
To stretch out main body of calf.

Facing and resting hands on wall – head up, back straight, abdominals in – place right foot in front of left with right foot approximately 6 inches from wall. Both heels remain flat on the floor, toes pointing forwards, as you ease pelvis forward to feel stretch in main body of left calf. Hold for 10–15 seconds, then repeat on other leg.

Lift one foot. Bend supporting leg. Slowly rotate foot one way, then the other. Repeat on other foot.

*Shoulder shrugs / rolls*

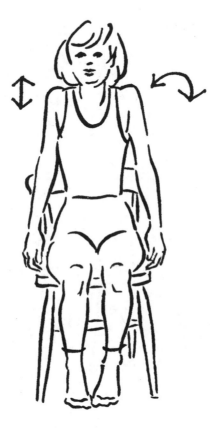

With arms relaxed, slowly lift shoulders upwards to ears and lower to floor. Repeat 4 times. Now press shoulders forward, separating shoulder blades, then squeeze backwards, shoulder blades together. Repeat 4 times. Repeat section twice.

*Upper back stretch*

Sit tall, grab one hand on top of other and press palms forward (arms extended in front). Separate shoulder blades, stretching across upper back. Hold 4 counts. (Relax chin down to chest with this stretch to gently lengthen and ease back of neck).

*Upper back and torso*

Looking straight ahead, take palms up towards ceiling and reach up to stretch upper back and waist. Hold 8–10 seconds.

Sitting tall, interlace fingers, take palms behind head (hands ½-inch away from head). Open elbows out wide, squeeze shoulder blades together and feel stretch across the chest. Hold 4 counts. Relax.

Sit back into chair, feet parallel, a little wider than shoulder width apart. Take arms above head, lengthening trunk of body. Keep abdominals pulled in and head and neck in line with spine. Slowly lower body forward, resting chest on to thighs while letting the head, neck and arms hang relaxed. Hold 6–8 counts. Slowly roll back up through the spine, with shoulders and head last to come up, back to your sitting position.

Sitting on a chair, lift one foot off floor, point toes forward and hold the stretch across top of foot for 4 counts. Now flex foot backwards, pulling toes back towards face, and hold 4 counts, feeling stretch behind lower leg. Slowly rotate foot, drawing a large circle one way then the other 4–6 times.

*Squats*

Holding on to back of chair for balance, turn toes outwards and stand tall, lifting through top of head. Tighten buttocks and lengthen leg muscles. Now slowly bend knees into a squat position (keeping hips just above knee level). Hold 5 counts, slowly stand tall and repeat. Feel stretch in hips, groin and inner thigh. Repeat 4 times.

# Three Times a Week

Strengthen and tone your muscles for great shape.

*Supported press-ups*
To strengthen arms and chest.

On all fours, place hands directly under shoulders, fingers facing forward. Pull in abdominals and tilt pelvis to straighten back. Keep hips placed above your knees as you bend elbows, lowering your forehead to the floor, then push up, straightening arms without locking into the elbow joints or rounding the shoulders. Keep the movement smooth with the head in line with the spine. Do 2–3 sets of 8.

*Upper body stretch*
To ease upper arm and shoulders.

From all fours, gently sit back over heels, keeping buttocks just above heels. Extend arms along the floor in front of you. Relax your head down and press palms into floor. Hold. Lengthen arms slightly more. Press palms again. Hold for 10–15 seconds.

*Triceps stretch*
To stretch and tone triceps.

Sit tall on floor, hold abdominals in and lengthen spine, legs in a comfortable position in front of you. Raise arms and bend right elbow. Rest right hand on upper back. Hold just above right elbow with left hand. Slowly lift head up and ease back against right arm until you feel a stretching sensation in the back of your right arm. Hold for 6 seconds. Repeat other side.

*Hip/outer thigh lifts*
To strengthen and tone hip and outer thigh.

Lie on side with hips, shoulders and head in a straight line. Bend both knees to a 90-degree angle, keeping them in line with your hips. Relax and let the upper body weight naturally fall forward. Hold abdominals in, back straight and top hip pressed forward. Lift and lower top leg, keeping knees in line, one above the other. Squeeze into outer thigh and hip as you lift. Repeat on other leg.

*Inner thigh squeeze*
To strengthen and tone inner thigh muscles.

Lying on your side as above, from both knees bent, slowly extend out and straighten lower leg in line with the upper body. Keeping the upper leg bent and relaxed forward, slowly lift and lower bottom leg a few inches, with the inside of your leg and foot facing the ceiling. Repeat 10 times. Repeat on other leg.

*Torso stretch*
To stretch lower back, outer thigh, hip and neck.

Lie on back, both knees bent, feet on floor. Gently drop both legs to one side as you extend both arms from chest level and lower to other side. Look towards your hands to release your neck. Hold for 5–10 seconds. Slowly lift knees and arms to centre. Repeat other side.

*Inner thigh stretch*
To release inner thighs.
Lie on your back, knees bent, hold abdominals in towards small of

back and press back into floor to prevent arching. Keep feet together as you slowly let the knees part and legs open towards floor. Relax and hold for 5–10 seconds.


*Pelvic tilt*
To strengthen abdominals.

Lie on your back, hands behind your head, knees bent, feet flat on floor, hip width apart. Pull in and flatten your tummy (abdominals) as you tilt the pelvis upwards and press lower back to the floor. There should be no space between the lower back and the floor as you adopt this position. Hold for 3 counts and release. Repeat 6 times.

*Abdominal curl*
To strengthen and tone abdominals.

Lie on your back, both knees bent, feet hip width apart and lower back pressed to the floor. With your hands behind your head, elbows out wide, ease head back into hands to support its weight. Now pull in and flatten tummy (abdominals) as you slowly lift head and shoulders 1 or 2 inches above the floor, then slowly lower. Keep head and neck in line with the spine. Chin up, head back and 'lift', leading with the chest. Exhale as you lift, inhale as you lower. Repeat 5–10 times.

*Waist toner*
To strengthen and tone waist.

This is performed as above but release left hand from behind head (right hand supporting weight of head). Keep left arm close to left side of body and face the ceiling. Gently reach left fingers towards left ankle and move directly to the side. Squeeze into left side of waist and release. For added resistance, raise shoulders slightly. Repeat.

*Knee hug*
To release tension in abdominals and ease out lower back.

Lie on floor, knees bent (as in previous exercise). Slowly bring your knees into chest. Holding underneath the knee joints, pull knees towards chest. The lower back and chest are relaxed to the floor. Hold for 10 seconds.

*Full body stretch*
To stretch abdominals, rib cage, spine, shoulders, arms and feet.

Lie on floor, knees bent. Slowly raise arms above head as you slide feet away to extend legs. Now point toes and fingers in opposite directions. To stop lower back from arching, slightly bend knees as you lengthen the whole body. Breathe deeply and gently increase the stretch as you exhale.

# Every Evening

*Deep relaxation*
Relax and unwind with total body relaxation.

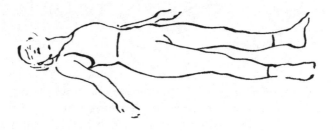

From the preceding abdominal stretch, slowly bring your hands down by your sides, palms facing ceiling. Let your feet relax outwards, roll your head to one side, close your eyes and relax. Let the whole body become heavy and 'melt' into the floor. With deep, steady breathing, try to empty your mind and let any thoughts drift away. Relax in this position for as long as you wish.

# The Fourth Way – Energy for Life: Planning a Stress-Free Diet

*Each one of the substances of a man's diet
acts upon his body and changes it in some way,
and upon these changes his whole life depends.*
HIPPOCRATES

## Getting the Right Balance

When we're under stress, our bodies use up nutrients faster and less efficiently than they normally do. And it's during these times that we tend to binge on unhealthy comfort foods which sabotage our bodies. To strengthen our body's defences against stress, and to eliminate harmful toxins, we need to eat more foods which are high in stress-busting nutrients, and fewer foods which contribute little or nothing to a nutritious diet.

A healthy diet is a low-stress diet, a nutritious, vitality-packed diet which provides the body with the energy it needs to cope with the stresses and strains of modern life. A well-balanced diet is the key to health, vitality and realistic weight control. Health guidelines both in the UK and in the USA urge us to cut down on fat, and balance this by eating more complex carbohydrates (bread, cereals, pasta, rice and potatoes). Scientific observation of the dietary habits of the healthiest people in the world show that more than 50 per cent of their diet is composed of these CC foods. It's from these findings that the Healthy Eating Pyramid evolved.

Destressing your diet is about rebalancing your eating habits, and the Healthy Eating Pyramid is the way to do this.

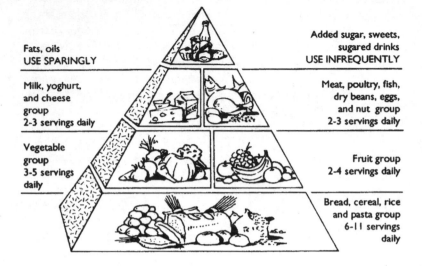

From the base to the apex, the main food groups occupy space according to their contribution to a healthy diet.

One serving is:

| | |
|---|---|
| 60–75g (2½–3 oz ) lean meat | 50 g (2 oz) raw vegetables |
| 40–50g (1½–2 oz ) cheese | 1 slice bread |
| 50 g (2 oz) cooked beans | 75 g (3 oz) rice, cereal or pasta |
| 150ml (6 fl oz) juice | 100–125 g (4–5 oz) white fish |

From the base to the apex, the main food groups occupy space according to their contribution to a healthy diet. Concentrate on giving a higher profile to foods on the first two levels of the pyramid – the CC foods, fruit and vegetables. These are the foods to eat most of and plan your meals around, ensuring that CC foods make up around 50–60 per cent of your meal, supplemented by generous quantities of fruit and vegetables.

Up to the top of the pyramid, meat and dairy products play a reducing role in a healthy diet, and fats, oils and sugars should be eaten sparingly. Aim to cut saturated fat by eating more white meat and fish and using low-fat dairy products – it's the fat in your diet that makes you fat! And cut down on 'added' sugar in the form of cakes, sweets, biscuits and sugared drinks. Always aim to eat fresh foods when possible and avoid or cut down on processed foods.

Everyone's dietary requirements are different, so you need to be creative and adapt the guidelines in the pyramid to match your own personal tastes and nutritional needs. Don't forget about exercise. Research shows that it's much easier to change eating habits and keep up a healthy diet if you also exercise. Exercise, such as brisk walking, gets those all-important circadian rhythms moving. It speeds up your metabolic rate and gives you the energy, focus and motivation to make the necessary changes in your diet.

The following recipes in 'Blueprint Menus for the Week' and 'Mix 'n' Match Recipes' are all based on the Healthy Eating Pyramid. By following the Blueprint Menus you will soon become familiar with stress-free eating – delicious foods to give you lots of energy and vitality. The Mix 'n' Match Recipes can then be used to maintain your stress-free diet. Choose foods that you like but make sure you balance your diet over the week. If a certain food is not available or you prefer, for example, a different type of fish, then adapt the recipes to suit yourself.

# Blueprint Menus for the Week

These recipes are for two people – simply multiply or halve amounts as required. One light meal and one main meal are given for each day. Eat fresh fruit after meals as desired – there are ideas for fresh fruit with a difference at the end of the Mix 'n' Match Recipes. Suggestions for *The Rhythm for Life* breakfasts are given at the end of the Energy for Life section.

# Menu for Monday

### Watercress and Feta Sandwich

2 pitta breads
watercress
1 medium tomato, thinly sliced
wedge of cucumber, thinly sliced
75 g (3 oz) feta cheese, thinly sliced
½ lemon
freshly ground black pepper

Arrange the sandwich filling inside the pitta bread. Squeeze some lemon juice into the sandwich and add some freshly ground black pepper.

### Thai Prawns

300 g (10 oz) uncooked tiger prawns, peeled
100 g (4 oz) mushrooms, sliced
2 cloves garlic, finely chopped
2-inch piece of lemon grass, squashed to release flavour
2 spring onions, shredded
10 ml (2 tsp) Nam Pla fish sauce
5 ml (1 tsp) chilli sauce
10 ml (2 tsp) sunflower oil

Heat the oil in a pan, add the mushrooms, garlic and lemon grass and cook for 3 minutes, stirring occasionally. Add the prawns, spring onions, fish sauce and chilli sauce and stir for about 2 minutes or until the prawns become pink. Remove the lemon grass and discard. Serve immediately with Thai fragrant or Basmati rice.

# Menu for Tuesday

### Spicy Rice Salad

100 g (4 oz) cooked rice
100 g (4 oz) cooked petits pois
1 medium carrot, sliced and cooked
2 shallots, finely chopped
2 small slices cooked ham, shredded
10 ml (2 tsp) low-fat mayonnaise
3 ml (½ tsp) chilli sauce
25 g (1 oz) flaked almonds
2 lemon wedges
freshly ground black pepper

Allow the cooked rice and vegetables to cool, then mix with the mayonnaise and chilli sauce. Stir in the shredded ham and arrange the salad on individual plates. Garnish with flaked almonds and a lemon wedge and add some freshly ground black pepper. Serve with wholemeal bread.

### Roasted Vegetable Pasta

1 medium green pepper
1 medium red pepper
1 medium red onion
1 medium aubergine
420 g (15 oz) tin chopped tomatoes
4 cloves garlic, finely chopped
5 ml (1 tsp) chopped fresh parsley or 3 ml (½ tsp) dried mixed
  herbs
1 mozzarella cheese, cut into small pieces
freshly grated Parmesan cheese
freshly ground sea salt and black pepper
150 g (6 oz) pasta

Cook the pasta as directed. Roast the green and red peppers, red onion and aubergine in a preheated oven, Gas Mark 6 (200C/400F), for 30–40 minutes, turning occasionally. Remove the skins from the vegetables and chop the flesh. Discard the skins but retain as much juice as possible. Put the chopped vegetables and juice into a pan with the chopped tomatoes, garlic, herbs and some freshly ground salt and pepper. Cook over a medium heat for about 5 minutes. Stir the mozzarella and Parmesan cheese into the vegetables. Put the pasta on individual plates and spoon the vegetables on to the pasta. Garnish with a few slivers of fresh Parmesan cheese. Serve immediately with a green salad.

# Menu for Wednesday

### *Asparagus and Kiwi Fruit Salad*

4 asparagus spears, lightly cooked
1 medium kiwi fruit
5 ml (1 tsp) low-fat mayonnaise
10 ml (2 tsp) low-fat natural yogurt
juice of ½ lemon
100 g (4 oz) cooked pasta
freshly ground black pepper

Cut the asparagus spears into 1-inch pieces. Remove the skin from the kiwi fruit and cut into small pieces. Mix the pasta with the mayonnaise, yogurt and lemon juice, then gently stir in the asparagus and kiwi fruit. Arrange on individual plates and add some freshly ground black pepper. Serve with wholemeal bread.

### *Mexican Turkey*

220 g (8 oz) minced turkey
1 medium red onion, chopped
2 cloves garlic, finely chopped
1 small red chilli pepper, seeds discarded, finely chopped
420 g (15 oz) tin chopped tomatoes
10 ml (2 tsp) tomato purée
100 g (4 oz) mushrooms, chopped
corn from 1 corn on the cob
220 g (8 oz) cooked red kidney beans
5 ml (1 tsp) chopped fresh parsley or 3 ml (½ tsp) dried mixed
  herbs
freshly ground sea salt and black pepper
150 g (6 oz) long grain rice
2 lime wedges

Cook the rice as directed. Put the minced turkey, red onion, garlic, chilli pepper, chopped tomatoes and tomato purée into a pan, stir well and cook over a medium heat for about 25 minutes, stirring occasionally. Add the mushrooms, corn, red kidney beans, herbs and some freshly ground salt and pepper and cook for a further 5 minutes. Stir in the cooked rice, then serve immediately, garnished with a lime wedge.

# Menu for Thursday

### Mozzarella and Salami Sandwich

1 mozzarella cheese, sliced
4 thin slices salami
1 medium tomato, sliced
4 fresh basil leaves
2 wedges baguette

Cut open the bread, leaving one side uncut. Arrange the mozzarella cheese, tomato, salami and basil leaves in the baguette and serve.

### Chinese Noodles with Fish

300 g (10 oz) white fish, with skin removed, cut into bite-sized
  pieces
1 medium green pepper, sliced
1 medium red pepper, sliced
100 g (4 oz) mushrooms, sliced
4 spring onions, shredded
10 ml (2 tsp) Nam Pla fish sauce
5 ml (1 tsp) soy sauce
¼-inch piece fresh root ginger, peeled and finely chopped
juice of ½ orange
3 ml (½ tsp) cornflour, mixed to a paste with cold water
10 ml (2 tsp) sunflower oil
25 g (1 oz) cashew nuts, halved
100 g (4 oz) egg noodles

Cook the noodles as directed on the packet. Heat the oil in a pan, add the green and red peppers and mushrooms and cook over a medium heat for about 5 minutes. Add the spring onions, fish sauce, soy sauce, ginger and orange juice, and mix together well. Stir in the cornflour and continue stirring for a few minutes to cook, adding a little water if necessary. Place the pieces of fish on top of the vegetables, cover the pan and cook for about 5 minutes. Check that the fish is cooked, taking care not to overcook. Arrange the noodles on individual plates, spoon over the fish and vegetables, garnish with the cashew nuts and serve immediately.

# Menu for Friday

### Tuna and Avocado Salad

220 g (8 oz) tin tuna in brine, drained and flaked
1 small ripe avocado
1 medium tomato, chopped
5 ml (1 tsp) low-fat mayonnaise
10 ml (2 tsp) low-fat natural yogurt
juice of ½ lemon
5 ml (1 tsp) sesame seeds
100 g (4 oz) cooked pasta
freshly ground black pepper

Cut the avocado in half, remove the skin and cut the avocado into small cubes. Mix the pasta with the mayonnaise, yogurt and lemon juice. Stir in the tuna and tomato, then add the avocado. Arrange on individual plates, then scatter the sesame seeds over the salad and add some freshly ground black pepper. Serve with wholemeal bread.

### Vegetable Curry

2 medium sweet potatoes, cleaned and cut into small pieces
100 g (4 oz) mushrooms, sliced
100 g (4 oz) frozen petits pois
1 medium head broccoli, cut into florets and the stem cubed
1 medium onion, chopped
2 cloves garlic, finely chopped
420 g (15 oz) tin chopped tomatoes
5 ml (1 tsp) tomato purée
10 ml (2 tsp) ground coriander
5 ml (1 tsp) ground cumin
10 ml (2 tsp) chilli sauce – or to taste
freshly ground sea salt and black pepper

Put the sweet potatoes into a large pan with the onion, garlic, chopped tomatoes and tomato purée and cook over a medium heat for about 10 minutes, stirring occasionally. Stir in the coriander, cumin, chilli sauce and some freshly ground salt and pepper, then add the mushrooms, petits pois and broccoli and cook for a further 10 minutes or until all the vegetables are cooked, taking care not to overcook them. Serve immediately with Basmati rice.

# Menu for Saturday

### Jacket Potato with Spinach and Bean Salad

2 baking potatoes
handful raw spinach leaves
150 g (6 oz) cooked white haricot beans
small wedge of cucumber, diced
5 ml (1 tsp) olive oil
5 ml (1 tsp) balsamic vinegar
freshly ground sea salt and black pepper

Bake the potatoes until soft inside but crisp outside. Meanwhile mix the olive oil, balsamic vinegar and some freshly ground salt and pepper. Add the beans and cucumber and stir. Cut open the potatoes lengthways and put on to individual plates. Arrange some spinach leaves on each plate and spoon the salad on to the leaves.

### Salmon with Mediterranean Vegetables

2 x 125 g (5 oz) fresh salmon fillets, skin removed
1 small bulb fennel, trimmed and cut into small pieces
1 medium onion, chopped
2 cloves garlic, finely chopped
1 medium green pepper, sliced
1 medium red pepper, sliced
2 medium courgettes, sliced diagonally
100 g (4 oz) mushrooms, sliced
420 g (15 oz) tin chopped tomatoes
10 ml (2 tsp) Nam Pla fish sauce
5 ml (1 tsp) chopped fresh dill or 3 ml (½ tsp) dried mixed herbs
freshly ground black pepper

Put the fennel, onion, garlic and chopped tomatoes into a pan and cook over a medium heat for about 10 minutes, stirring occasionally. Add the green and red peppers, courgettes, mushrooms, fish sauce, herbs and some freshly ground black pepper and cook for a further 5 minutes. Place the salmon fillets on top of the vegetables, cover the pan and cook for about 5 minutes. Check that the fish is cooked, taking care not to overcook. Arrange the vegetables on individual plates and place the salmon on top. Serve immediately with a green salad.

# Menu for Sunday

### Cheese and Chive Omelette

100 g (4 oz) Edam cheese, grated
10 ml (2 tsp) chopped fresh chives
4 large eggs
10 ml (2 tsp) olive oil
freshly ground sea salt and black pepper

Whisk the eggs with a little water or milk and some freshly ground salt and pepper. Add the chives. Heat the oil in a frying pan, add the eggs and cook until the omelette is almost set. Scatter the grated cheese over the omelette and put under a preheated grill for a few moments. Fold over the omelette, cut in half and arrange on individual plates garnished with some whole chives. Serve immediately with wholemeal bread.

### Normandy Pork

220 g (8 oz) pork fillet, cut into bite-sized pieces
4 shallots, chopped
300 ml (10 fl oz) dry cider
100 g (4 oz) mushrooms, sliced
5 ml (1 tsp) chopped fresh parsley or 3 ml (½ tsp) dried mixed herbs
5 ml (1 tsp) mustard
125 ml (5 fl oz) low-fat single cream
freshly ground sea salt and black pepper

Put the pork with the shallots and cider into a pan, cover and cook over a medium heat for 20–25 minutes. Add the mushrooms and herbs and cook for a further 5 minutes. Reduce the liquid to about 15 ml (1 tbsp), then add the mustard, cream and some freshly ground salt and pepper and heat thoroughly. Serve immediately with new potatoes and red cabbage with apple.

# Mix 'n' Match Recipes for the Month

Now you have completed your Blueprint Menus for the Week, continue your stress-free diet for the rest of the month by selecting recipes from the following section. Mix 'n' match them with the previous recipes, referring to the Healthy Eating Pyramid as a guide.

## Fish and Shellfish

### Tuna and Prawn Kebabs

220 g (8 oz) fresh tuna, cut into cubes
8 raw tiger prawns, shelled
4 shallots, peeled and halved
8 small mushrooms
olive oil
freshly ground black pepper
2 lemon wedges

Soak 4 6-inch wooden kebab sticks in water for about 30 minutes to prevent burning. Arrange the tuna, prawns, shallots and mushrooms on the kebab sticks. Brush with olive oil and grind some black pepper on to the kebabs. Grill for about 5 minutes, turning to cook evenly. Serve garnished with a lemon wedge.

### Monkfish with Mustard and Cream Sauce

2 fillets of monkfish, skin removed
1 medium onion, chopped
100 g (4 oz) petits pois
100 g (4 oz) white mushrooms, sliced
3 ml (½ tsp) mustard
10 ml (2 tsp) Nam Pla fish sauce
125 ml (5 fl oz) low-fat single cream
freshly ground black pepper

Put the onion and petits pois in a large pan with 300 ml (10 fl oz) water and cook over a medium heat for about 5 minutes. Stir in the mushrooms, mustard and fish sauce and a little more water if necessary. Lay the monkfish fillets on top of the vegetables, cover the pan and cook for a further 5 minutes. Reduce the liquid to about 15 ml (1 tbsp). Stir in the cream, taking care not to break the fish, and add some freshly ground black pepper. Heat thoroughly, then serve immediately.

---

*The Rhythm for Life* Superfood – **Onions**
Natural antibiotic action, can help relieve bronchial constriction and reduce risk of heart disease, strokes and cancer

---

### Spicy Cod

2 x 125 g (5 oz) fillets of cod, skin removed
4 shallots, chopped
2 cloves garlic, finely chopped
1 small red chilli pepper, seeds removed and finely chopped
juice of ½ lemon
10 ml (2 tsp) Nam Pla fish sauce
10 ml (2 tsp) olive oil
freshly ground black pepper

Heat the oil in a pan, add the shallots, garlic and chilli pepper and cook over a medium heat for about 5 minutes. Mix together the lemon juice, fish sauce and chilli sauce, then stir in, adding a little water if necessary. Put the cod fillets into the pan, cover and cook for 7–8 minutes, stirring to prevent sticking but taking care not to break the fish. Add some freshly ground black pepper and serve immediately.

---

*The Rhythm for Life* Superfood – **Chilli Peppers**
Aid digestion, help clear congestion in airways, stimulate circulation and may help prevent blood clots

---

## Kedgeree

300 g (10 oz) smoked haddock, preferably undyed, skin removed
1 medium onion, chopped
150 g (6 oz) rice, Basmati or long grain
2 eggs, hard boiled and quartered
5 ml (1 tsp) ground coriander
3 ml (½ tsp) ground turmeric
5 ml (1 tsp) chopped fresh parsley or 3 ml (½ tsp) dried mixed herbs
freshly ground sea salt and black pepper

Poach the smoked haddock with the onion in water for about 8 minutes. Remove the fish and onion from the water, flake the fish and keep warm. Cook the rice for the time directed, using the cooking liquid and extra water as required and adding the coriander and turmeric. Drain the rice, then stir in the fish, onion, herbs and some freshly ground salt and pepper. Serve immediately, garnished with the quarters of egg.

## Spaghetti Marinara

125 g (5 oz) prawns, peeled
300 g (10 oz) tin clams, drained
420 g (15 oz) tin chopped tomatoes
2 shallots, finely chopped
1 clove garlic, finely chopped
100 g (4 oz) mushrooms, sliced
10 ml (2 tsp) Nam Pla fish sauce
5 ml (1 tsp) chopped fresh dill or 3 ml (½ tsp) dried mixed herbs
freshly ground black pepper
150 g (6 oz) spaghetti

Cook the spaghetti as directed. Put the chopped tomatoes, shallots and garlic into a pan and cook over a medium heat for about 5 minutes, stirring occasionally. Add the mushrooms, fish sauce, herbs and black pepper and cook for a further 5 minutes. Stir in the prawns and clams and heat thoroughly. Serve the spaghetti on individual plates with the marinara sauce poured over. Garnish with a sprig of dill.

## Pasta with Smoked Salmon and Prawns

100 g (4 oz) smoked salmon
150 g (6 oz) prawns, peeled
4 shallots, chopped
2 cloves garlic, finely chopped
100 g (4 oz) petits pois
100 g (4 oz) white mushrooms, sliced
10 ml (2 tsp) Nam Pla fish sauce
5 ml (1 tsp) chopped fresh dill or 3 ml (½ tsp) dried mixed herbs
125 ml (5 fl oz) low-fat single cream
freshly ground black pepper
150 g (6 oz) pasta

Cook the pasta as directed. Put the shallots, garlic and petits pois into a large pan with 300 ml (10 fl oz) water and cook over a medium heat for 5 minutes. Stir in the mushrooms, fish sauce and herbs and cook for a further 5 minutes. Reduce the liquid to about 15 ml (1 tbsp). Add the smoked salmon, prawns, cream and some black pepper and heat thoroughly. Serve the pasta on individual plates with the sauce spooned over. Garnish with a sprig of dill.

> *The Rhythm for Life* Superfood – **Peas (petits pois)**
> Rich in soluble fibre, rich in proteins, richest food source of vitamin B1; can help steady blood sugar and energy levels, may help reduce risk of heart disease

## Sardines with Green and Red Peppers

6 fresh sardines, gutted and descaled
1 small green pepper, diced
1 small red pepper, diced
2 shallots, chopped
1 clove garlic, finely chopped
10 ml (2 tsp) olive oil
juice of ½ lemon
freshly ground black pepper

Heat the olive oil in a pan and cook the sardines, shallots and garlic over a medium heat for 10 minutes, turning to cook evenly. Add the diced green and red peppers, lemon juice and some freshly ground black pepper, cook for about two minutes and serve immediately.

---

*The Rhythm for Life* Superfood – **Oily Fish**
Omega–3 fatty acids in oily fish linked to a wide range of health benefits; lower risk of heart disease, stroke, may lower risk of cancer, can help inflammatory skin conditions and rheumatoid arthritis

---

# Meat

### Chicken, Lentils and Chorizo

2 chicken breast fillets, skin removed, cut into bite-sized pieces
220 g (8 oz) cooked lentils
2 small Chorizo sausages, cut into small pieces
1 medium red onion, chopped
2 cloves garlic, chopped
1 small red chilli pepper, seeds removed, finely chopped
420 g (15 oz) tin chopped tomatoes
freshly ground sea salt and black pepper

Put the chicken, onion, garlic, chilli pepper and tomatoes into a large pan and cook over a medium heat for about 25 minutes, or until the chicken is cooked, stirring occasionally and adding a little water if necessary. Stir in the lentils, Chorizo sausage and some salt and pepper and heat thoroughly.

---

*The Rhythm for Life* Superfood – **Lentils and Beans**
Good source of fibre, potassium, iron and folate; help prevent anaemia and can reduce risk of heart disease

---

## Persian Chicken

2 chicken breast fillets, skin removed, cut into bite-sized pieces
1 medium onion, chopped
2 cloves garlic, finely chopped
10 ml (2 tsp) vegetable oil
150 g (6 oz) long grain rice
3 ml (½ tsp) cinnamon powder
50 g (2 oz) sultanas
juice of ½ orange
25 g (1 oz) flaked toasted almonds
freshly ground sea salt and black pepper

Cook the rice as directed, then drain and keep warm. Meanwhile heat the oil in a large pan, add the chicken, onion and garlic and cook over a medium heat for about 20 minutes, stirring occasionally and adding water a little at a time to keep the meat moist. When the chicken is almost cooked, add the cooked rice, cinnamon, sultanas, orange juice and some freshly ground salt and pepper, and stir to mix together all ingredients. Serve garnished with the toasted almonds.


## Turkey Vilao

4 turkey breast steaks
1 medium onion, chopped
2 medium potatoes
150 g (6 oz) broccoli
1 large egg, hard-boiled and quartered
5 ml (1 tsp) chopped fresh parsley or 3 ml (½ tsp) dried mixed
  herbs
10 ml (2 tsp) wine vinegar
125 ml (5 fl oz) white wine
10 ml (2 tsp) olive oil
freshly ground sea salt and black pepper

Boil the potatoes and cut into ½-inch rounds. Cut the broccoli into bite-sized pieces and cook lightly. Heat the olive oil in a pan, add the turkey and onion and cook for about 20 minutes, turning to cook evenly. Add the wine vinegar, wine, herbs and some freshly ground salt and pepper to the turkey and heat through for a few moments. Arrange the potatoes, broccoli and hard-boiled egg on individual plates, then put the turkey on to the vegetables, spoon over the sauce and serve immediately.

---

*The Rhythm for Life* Superfood – **Broccoli**
Rich in antioxidants, folate, iron and calcium; can help reduce
risk of heart disease, stroke, cancer and cataracts

---

### Spicy Beef with Courgettes

220 g (8 oz) fillet steak
2 medium courgettes, sliced diagonally
4 shallots, chopped
2 cloves garlic, finely chopped
½-inch piece fresh root ginger, peeled and finely chopped
10 ml (2 tsp) olive oil
5 ml (1 tsp) chilli sauce
10 ml (2 tsp) soy sauce
juice of ½ lemon
freshly ground sea salt and black pepper

Cut the steak into thin slices, about ½-inch wide by 1 inch. Heat the oil in a large pan and add the shallots, garlic, ginger and steak. Cook over a medium heat for about 5 minutes, stirring to prevent sticking. Add the courgettes and cook for a further 5 minutes, adding a little water if necessary. Mix together the chilli sauce, soy sauce and lemon juice, pour over the meat and heat thoroughly. Add some freshly ground salt and pepper and stir to mix together all ingredients.

---

*The Rhythm for Life* Superfood – **Ginger**
Aids digestion, reduces tendency to blood clots, helps fight
colds, may help relieve rheumatism

---

## Lamb with Aubergine

220 g (8 oz) lean lamb, minced
1 medium aubergine, diced
4 shallots, chopped
2 cloves garlic, finely chopped
420 g (15 oz) tin chopped tomatoes
100 g (4 oz) mushrooms, sliced
5 ml (1 tsp) chilli sauce
125 g (5 oz) low-fat natural yogurt
5 ml (1 tsp) chopped fresh mint or 3 ml (½ tsp) dried mixed herbs
freshly ground sea salt and black pepper

Put the minced lamb, shallots, garlic and chopped tomatoes into a large pan and cook over a medium heat for about 25 minutes, stirring occasionally and adding a little water if necessary. Meanwhile put the diced aubergine into another pan, cover with boiling water and simmer for about 10 minutes, then drain and keep warm. Add the mushrooms, chilli sauce, yogurt, herbs and some freshly ground salt and pepper to the lamb and cook for a further 5 minutes, then add the aubergine and stir to mix together all ingredients.

> The Rhythm for Life Superfood – **Yogurt**
> Has high nutritional value but 'live' yogurt has extra therapeutic benefits; aids immune system

## Guinea Fowl with Mushrooms

2 guinea fowl breast fillets, skin removed (this recipe also works
  well with chicken)
4 shallots, chopped
2 cloves garlic, finely chopped
2 medium carrots, thinly sliced
100 g (4 oz) mushrooms, sliced
10 ml (2 tsp) olive oil
300 ml (10 fl oz) white wine and water mixed
10 ml (2 tsp) Nam Pla fish sauce
125 ml (5 fl oz) low-fat single cream

5 ml (1 tsp) chopped fresh chives or 3 ml (½ tsp) dried mixed herbs
freshly ground black pepper

Heat the olive oil in a large pan and add the guinea fowl, shallots
and garlic. Cook over a medium heat for 10 minutes, turning the
meat to cook evenly. Add the carrots and the wine and water, cover
and cook for a further 10 minutes. Add the mushrooms, fish sauce
and herbs and cook for 5 minutes. Check that the meat is cooked
through, then reduce the liquid to about 15 ml (1 tbsp). Stir in the
cream and some freshly ground black pepper and heat thoroughly.
Serve immediately, garnished with a few whole chives.

---

*The Rhythm for Life* Superfood – **Carrots**
Rich in carotenes, source of vitamins and fibre; can reduce risk
of cancer, can lower cholesterol and help prevent food poisoning

---

### Pork Fillet with Sautéed Cabbage

220 g (8 oz) pork fillet
wedge of cabbage, shredded
10 ml (2 tsp) olive oil
125 ml (5 fl oz) red wine
juice of ½ lemon
freshly ground sea salt and black pepper

Put the pork fillet into an ovenproof dish with the red wine and
lemon juice and bake in a preheated oven, Gas Mark 6
(200C/400F), for about 40 minutes, or until tender. About 15
minutes before the pork is cooked, steam the shredded cabbage for
about 8 minutes, then heat the olive oil in a pan and sauté the
cabbage for a few minutes, stirring to prevent sticking. Add some
freshly ground salt and pepper. Remove the pork from the oven
and cut into medallions. Arrange the cabbage on individual plates,
place the pork medallions on to the cabbage, spoon over the wine
sauce and serve immediately.

> *The Rhythm for Life* Superfood – **Cabbage**
> Good source of vitamins, minerals, fibre, folate, antioxidants;
> helps ulcers, aids digestive health, can reduce risk of heart disease,
> strokes, cancer and cataracts

# *Vegetarian*

### *Pasta Siciliana*

1 medium aubergine, cut into cubes
4 shallots, chopped
2 cloves garlic, finely chopped
300 ml (10 fl oz) tomato passata
100 g (4 oz) mushrooms, sliced
½ mozzarella cheese, diced
5 ml (1 tsp) chilli sauce
10 ml (2 tsp) fresh basil, torn into pieces
freshly ground sea salt and black pepper
150 g (6 oz) pasta

Cook the pasta as directed. Put the aubergine, shallots, garlic and
tomato passata into a pan and cook over a medium heat for about
5 minutes. Add the mushrooms and cook for a further 5 minutes.
Stir in the mozzarella, chilli sauce, basil and some freshly ground
salt and pepper. Serve the pasta on individual plates with the sauce
poured over. Garnish with a few black olives.

> *The Rhythm for Life* Superfood – **Garlic**
> Probably the best known healing food, helps circulation, fights
> infection, helps reduce cholesterol level, high blood pressure and
> possibly risk of cancer

### *Bean Ragout*

125 g (5 oz) cooked red kidney beans
125 g (5 oz) cooked green lima or broad beans
125 g (5 oz) cooked soya beans

1 large onion, chopped
2 cloves garlic, finely chopped
100 g (4 oz) mushrooms, sliced
1 small green pepper, diced
1 small red pepper, diced
420 g (15 oz) tin chopped tomatoes
5 ml (1 tsp) tomato purée
10 ml (2 tsp) soy sauce
1 bouquet garni or 5 ml (1 tsp) dried mixed herbs
freshly ground sea salt and black pepper

Put the onion, garlic, tomatoes, tomato purée and herbs into a large pan and cook over a medium heat for 5 minutes. Add the mushrooms and green and red peppers and cook for a further 5 minutes, adding some water if necessary. Stir in the beans and soy sauce, add some freshly ground salt and pepper and heat thoroughly.

---

*The Rhythm for Life* Superfood – **Soya Beans**
Rich in fibre, iron, calcium and potassium; help improve intestinal and heart health

---

### Baked Fennel

2 medium fennel bulbs
1 medium onion, chopped
2 cloves garlic, finely chopped
100 g (4 oz) mushrooms, sliced
420 g (15 oz) tin chopped tomatoes
5 ml (1 tsp) chopped fresh parsley or 3 ml (½ tsp) dried mixed herbs
10 ml (2 tsp) olive oil
freshly ground sea salt and black pepper

Trim the fennel and cut into quarters. Heat the oil in a pan and cook the fennel, onion and garlic over a medium heat for 5 minutes, stirring to prevent sticking. Put the fennel, onion and garlic into an ovenproof dish with the mushrooms, tomatoes, herbs and salt and pepper, and bake in a preheated oven, Gas Mark 6 (200C/400F), for about 30 minutes. Serve immediately.

> ## The Rhythm for Life Superfood – **Fennel**
> Helps digestion, can ease colic and intestinal cramp, can help avoid and reduce high blood pressure

### Leek and Egg Mornay

440 g (1 lb) leeks
2 large eggs, hard-boiled
1 medium onion, chopped
150 g (6 oz) Edam cheese, grated
300 ml (10 fl oz) milk
15 g (½ oz) cornflour, mixed to a paste with a little water
freshly ground sea salt and black pepper

Trim and clean the leeks, then cut into 3-inch pieces. Cook the leeks with the onion in a little water or by steaming for about 10 minutes. Drain thoroughly, then put into an ovenproof dish, arrange slices of hard-boiled egg on top and add some freshly ground salt and pepper. Bring the milk to the boil and stir in the cornflour. Simmer, stirring continuously for about 3 minutes, then stir in most of the grated cheese. Pour the sauce over the leeks and eggs, scatter the remaining grated cheese on top, then bake in a preheated oven, Gas Mark 6 (200C/400F), for 15 minutes. Brown under the grill for a few moments and serve immediately.

### Sweet and Sour Courgettes, Mushrooms and Peppers

2 large courgettes, sliced
100 g (4 oz) mushrooms, sliced – oyster mushrooms, if possible
1 medium green pepper, sliced
1 medium red pepper, sliced
2 spring onions, shredded
10 ml (2 tsp) vegetable oil
5 ml (1 tsp) wine vinegar
10 ml (2 tsp) soy sauce
5 ml (1 tsp) clear honey
juice of ½ orange

Heat the oil in a large pan and add the courgettes, mushrooms and green and red peppers. Cook over a medium heat for about 5 minutes. Add the wine vinegar, soy sauce, honey and orange juice, then stir in the shredded spring onions. Serve immediately.

### Aubergine with Melted Mozzarella

4 round slices of aubergine, each ½-inch thick
1 large tomato
mozzarella cheese
15 ml (1 tbsp) olive oil
10 ml (2 tsp) balsamic vinegar
fresh basil leaves
freshly ground sea salt and black pepper

Brush the aubergine slices with olive oil, then put under a preheated grill for about 5 minutes each side or until golden. Cut 4 slices of tomato, then put a slice on each piece of aubergine and grill for about 2 minutes. Cut 4 slices of mozzarella, put on top of each slice of tomato and grill for a few moments. Meanwhile, gently heat the remaining olive oil with the balsamic vinegar and some freshly ground salt and pepper. Serve immediately with the warm dressing spooned over and garnished with some fresh basil leaves.

### Celery and Mushroom Stir Fry

4 sticks celery, chopped
220 g (8 oz) mushrooms, sliced – mixed varieties, if possible
1 clove garlic, finely chopped
2 spring onions, shredded
10 ml (2 tsp) vegetable oil
10 ml (2 tsp) soy sauce
5 ml (1 tsp) chilli sauce
100 g (4 oz) rice, Basmati or long grain
10 ml (2 tsp) chopped cashews

Cook the rice as directed, drain and keep warm. Meanwhile heat the oil in a large pan and stir fry the celery, mushrooms and garlic for about 5 minutes. Add the soy sauce and chilli sauce, then stir in the shredded spring onions and cooked rice. Serve immediately with the chopped cashews scattered over the vegetables and rice.

*The Rhythm for Life* Superfood – **Celery**
Greener celery has more vitamin C, carotenes and folate; can help control blood pressure, has diuretic effect and calming effect

# Salads and Light Meals

### Watercress, Pear and Blue Cheese Salad

watercress
2 ripe pears, quartered
75 g (3 oz) blue cheese
½ lemon
freshly ground black pepper

Arrange the watercress on individual plates. Lay the pear quarters on the watercress and squeeze some lemon juice over the fruit. Crumble the blue cheese over the pears and add some freshly ground black pepper.

*The Rhythm for Life* Superfood – **Watercress**
Good source of iron, calcium, zinc, folate, vitamin C; helps prevent infections and anaemia, good for skin problems

### Avocado, Spinach and Orange Salad

1 ripe avocado
handful of raw spinach leaves, rinsed and dried
1 orange, peeled, segmented and skin removed
juice of ½ orange
freshly ground black pepper

Arrange the spinach leaves on individual plates. Cut the avocado in half and remove the skin. Cut the avocado halves into 5 or 6 strips and arrange on the bed of spinach with the orange segments. Spoon the freshly squeezed orange juice on to the avocado and add some freshly ground black pepper.

---

The *Rhythm for Life* Superfood – **Spinach**
Rich in antioxidants, potassium, folate, useful source of iron; may protect against eye degeneration, may reduce risk of cancer, can help prevent and relieve anaemia

---

### Spicy Fish Salad

100 g (4 oz) cooked white crab meat
100 g (4 oz) cooked prawns, peeled
1 small red onion, finely chopped
1 small green pepper, diced
4 radicchio leaves
10 ml (2 tsp) low-fat mayonnaise
5 ml (1 tsp) chilli sauce
juice of ½ lime
freshly ground sea salt and black pepper
2 lime wedges

Mix together the mayonnaise, chilli sauce, lime juice and salt and pepper. Add the crab meat, prawns, onion and green pepper and stir gently to coat with the dressing. Put 2 radicchio leaves on each plate and spoon the salad into the leaves. Garnish with a lime wedge.

### Roast Pepper Salad

1 medium green pepper
1 medium red pepper
1 medium orange or yellow pepper
5 ml (1 tsp) olive oil
5 ml (1 tsp) balsamic vinegar
freshly ground black pepper

Roast the peppers whole in a preheated oven, Gas Mark 6 (200C/400F), for about 40 minutes, turning every 10 minutes to cook evenly. Remove the skins (which will probably be charred) by putting the peppers into a closed poly bag for a few minutes, then gently pulling the skin from the flesh. Discard skins. Cut each pepper into half, discard seeds but retain juice and mix it with the olive oil and balsamic vinegar. Arrange one piece of green, red and orange or yellow pepper on to two plates. Spoon over the dressing and add some freshly ground black pepper.

> *The Rhythm for Life* Superfood – **Peppers**
> All peppers are rich in vitamin C and red ones are rich in carotenes, offering antioxidant protection

### Crab and Dill Omelette

1 dressed crab
10 ml (2 tsp) chopped fresh dill
4 large eggs
10 ml (2 tsp) olive oil
freshly ground sea salt and black pepper

Whisk the eggs with a little water or milk and salt and pepper. Add the dill and stir in the brown crab meat. Heat the oil in a frying pan, add the eggs and cook until the omelette is almost set. Arrange the white crab meat evenly over the omelette, then continue cooking for a few moments. Fold over the omelette and cut in half. Serve garnished with a sprig of dill.

### Baked Sweet Potato with Melted Cheese

2 sweet potatoes
2 medium tomatoes
100 g (4 oz) Cheddar cheese, grated
fresh basil leaves
freshly ground black pepper

Bake the potatoes until soft inside but crisp outside. Cut each tomato into 4 slices, then cut the sweet potatoes lengthways and put 2 slices of tomato on to each potato half. Scatter the grated cheese on top of the tomato slices and grill for a few moments until the cheese has melted. Add some freshly ground black pepper and garnish with fresh basil leaves.

---

*The Rhythm for Life* Superfood – **Sweet Potato**
Low-fat source of high vitamin E level, rich in antioxidants, source of potassium and iron; helps heart and skin health, helps regulate high blood pressure

---

### Feta and Tomato Salad

2 cos lettuce leaves, shredded
2 medium tomatoes, sliced
100 g (4 oz) feta cheese
8 black olives
freshly ground black pepper
2 lime wedges

Arrange the lettuce on individual plates with the tomato slices. Crumble the feta cheese over the salad and add the olives and some freshly ground black pepper. Garnish with lime wedges.

---

*The Rhythm for Life* Superfood – **Tomatoes**
Rich in antioxidants, may contain other protective substances

---

# Sweets

### Exotic Fruit Salad

½ mango
½ papaya
small bunch grapes
1 kiwi fruit
1 passion fruit

juice of 1 orange
2 fresh mint leaves

Cut the flesh from the mango and papaya, discarding all seeds, and cut into pieces. Cut the grapes into halves. Remove the skin from the kiwi fruit and cut the flesh into pieces. Cut the passion fruit in half and scoop out the flesh and seeds. Mix together all the fruits with the orange juice and serve in individual dishes garnished with a fresh mint leaf.

### Fruit Brochettes

small wedge of pineapple
2 kiwi fruit
1 peach
8 strawberries
½ lemon
3 ml (½ tsp) cinnamon powder

Cut the pineapple flesh from the skin and remove the skin from the kiwi fruit. Cut each of the pineapple, kiwi fruit and peach into eight pieces. Using 6-inch kebab sticks, arrange all the fruit to make 4 brochettes. Serve with lemon juice squeezed over the brochettes and dusted with a little cinnamon.

> *The Rhythm for Life* Superfood – **Citrus Fruits**
> Good source of vitamin C, potassium and folate; help prevent infection and reduce blood cholesterol levels

### Marinated Apricots

6 fresh apricots, halved
150 ml (6 fl oz) dessert wine
25 g (1 oz) flaked almonds, toasted

Marinate the apricot halves in the dessert wine for at least 30 minutes in the refrigerator. Serve in individual dishes with the toasted almonds scattered on top.

> ## The Rhythm for Life Superfood – **Apricots**
> Rich in fibre, potassium, beta-carotene; can help regulate blood pressure

### Pears in Red Wine

2 large pears
300 ml (10 fl oz) red wine
10 ml (2 tsp) clear honey
5 ml (1 tsp) cinnamon powder

Peel the pears, leaving their shape intact. Put them in a small pan with the red wine, cover and poach gently for about 12 minutes. Stir in the honey and cinnamon for the last 2 minutes of cooking time. The pears may be served hot or chilled.

### Pineapple with Kirsch

2 wedges pineapple, with leaves intact
15 ml (1 tbsp) kirsch
2 fresh mint leaves

Cut the pineapple flesh loose and then into 4 pieces, but leave on skin for serving. Add a few drops of kirsch to each piece of fruit. Serve garnished with a fresh mint leaf.

### Apple Yogurt

2 sweet apples
220 g (8 oz) low-fat natural yogurt
10 ml (2 tsp) clear honey

Cut the apples into quarters and core, leaving the skin on, then grate. Mix together the grated apples, yogurt and honey. Put into individual dishes and serve chilled.

> The Rhythm for Life Superfood – **Apples**
> Can help resistance to illness, aid digestion and disposal of
> unwanted substances, can help lower blood cholesterol levels

**Oranges in Grand Marnier**

2 medium oranges
juice of ½ orange
15 ml (1 tbsp) Grand Marnier

Peel the oranges and slice as thinly as possible, retaining the juice.
Mix together the orange juice and Grand Marnier. Serve the
oranges in individual dishes with the orange juice and Grand
Marnier spooned over.

# Energy for Life

## Seven ways to increase carbohydrate and fibre

- eat lots of fresh fruit and vegetables
- leave skins on apples, pears, potatoes
- eat more rice, particularly wholegrain or brown
- eat more pasta – but not too many rich sauces!
- choose from the huge range of bread now widely available
- use more cereals, such as couscous, bulgar, polenta
- eat more lentils and beans

## Seven ways to cut down on fat

- eat fresh rather than processed foods
- eat more fish and white meat rather than red meat
- choose lean meat and remove fat wherever possible
- use semi-skimmed or skimmed milk
- eat tomato-based rather than cream-based sauces
- use lemon- or yogurt-based salad dressings instead of mayonnaise
- use herbs and spices to enhance the flavour of vegetables instead of butter

## Seven ways to top up on vitamins and minerals

- eat some raw foods every day, particularly salads and fresh fruit
- choose foods that are really fresh from shops with a high turnover
- simply clean fruit and vegetables instead of peeling them if possible
- prepare fruit and vegetables immediately before eating or cooking them
- don't leave fruit or vegetables in water
- steam vegetables if possible, or use a minimum amount of water
- eat wholegrain foods as much as possible

## Seven ways to enjoy delicious soft drinks

- sparkling mineral water with ice and a twist of lime
- juice of ½ lemon topped up with chilled mineral water
- freshly squeezed orange juice
- freshly juiced carrots, apples and kiwi fruit
- tomato juice with a dash of Worcestershire sauce and a sprig of mint
- juice of ½ lemon and one orange topped up with sparkling ginger
- freshly squeezed pink grapefruit juice

## Seven ways to eat out healthily

- choose dishes that are not too high in fats and sugar
- choose grilled, poached or steamed foods
- eat fish or white meat
- avoid thick, creamy sauces which are laden with calories
- ask for vegetables not to be covered in butter
- ask to add salad dressing yourself to avoid having too much
- choose fruit rather than chocolate or creamy sweets

## Seven ways to prepare smart snacks

- fresh fruit, cut into bite-sized pieces or segments for ease

- crudités – raw vegetables cut into bite-sized pieces
- fresh juices – orange, grapefruit, carrot and apple
- low-fat natural yogurt, with fresh fruit added if wished
- dried fruit – apricots, dates, mango slices
- unsalted nuts – almonds, hazelnuts, brazils, walnuts – but not too many!
- seeds – pumpkin, sunflower, sesame – but again watch out for too many calories!

## Seven ways to start the day – The Rhythm for Life Breakfasts

The following are each for one person:

- glass of fresh grapefruit juice
  wholemeal toast with slices of grilled tomato

- bowl of bran flakes
  wholemeal toast with poached egg

- ½ grapefruit
  porridge with 10 ml (2 tsp) honey

- glass of fresh orange juice
  wholemeal toast with baked beans

- ½ pink grapefruit
  wholemeal toast with scrambled egg

- bowl of home-made muesli
  cooked ham with wholemeal bread

- glass of cranberry juice
  wholemeal toast with grilled mushrooms

The following market and store-cupboard lists will help you plan your shopping lists for a stress-free diet:

# Market List

## Vegetables

broccoli
cabbage
onions
beans – green, broad, etc.
green and red peppers
potatoes
carrots
celeriac
cauliflower
pumpkin
tomatoes
salad leaves
garlic

spinach
Brussels sprouts
chilli peppers
peas
aubergine
sweet potatoes
celery
asparagus
courgettes
squash
watercress
root ginger
herbs – parsley, dill, chives, basil, etc.

## Fruit

apples
kiwi fruit
mango
apricots
oranges
pineapple
nectarines

pomegranates
grapes
papaya
pears
bananas
peaches
avocado

## Fish

salmon
haddock
sole
prawns
herring
sardines

cod
monkfish
plaice
kippers
mackerel
tuna

## Meat

chicken breast fillets
guinea fowl breast fillets
lamb mince
fillet steak

turkey mince
pork fillet
lamb steaks

# Store-Cupboard List

nuts – cashews, walnuts, brazils, almonds, etc.
seeds – sesame, pumpkin, sunflower, etc.
dried apricots
tomato purée
tinned chopped tomatoes
dried mixed herbs
dried or tinned red kidney beans
dried or tinned lentils
dried or tinned soya beans
sea salt
black peppercorns
olive oil
vinegar
balsamic vinegar
mustard
Nam Pla fish sauce
chilli sauce
spices – ground coriander, cumin, turmeric, chilli powder, etc.

# PART THREE

# Reflection

*We must be still*
*and still moving*
*into another intensity.*
T.S. ELIOT, *FOUR QUARTETS*

*Time is the great physician.*
BENJAMIN DISRAELI

# The Fifth Way – Turning off to Tune in

*Get out of your mind at least once a day.*
ALAN WATTS

It was reported in *The Times* of London that the head of one of the world's largest corporations sent his staff a simple message: if they wanted to communicate with him, in future they should do it electronically – they should e-mail him. He said: 'When I set out to communicate, I want instant gratification. If I get any kind of delay I am frustrated; anything over 30 seconds can become very irritating.' This man sounds a real pain to himself and others, but his stressful behaviour indicates how technology is changing the way we all live and work.

Electronic mail, or e-mail, began making everyone's life easier, but there are reports that in some companies people are receiving 40 to 50 e-mails daily and in some cases more than 100. And, of course, it all has to be read and actioned. And that's in addition to telephone calls, voice mail, mobile phone calls and the fax. On the information superhighway, life is never dull.

But increasing numbers of overworked and overstretched executives and employees are more tense, nervous, anxious and stressed than they have ever been. And that goes for the rest of us too, whether we're teleworkers, at home looking after the kids, or retired. We never really relax. And when we do try to relax, what do many of us do? We 'work out' in the gym, we jog five miles before work, we take up action sports like bungee-jumping or hang-gliding. Our conscious minds are still churning away. We never rest. We never really switch off. And when we try to, we find it difficult to relax and completely let go. One reason for this is that we spend too much time inside our own heads.

## Head off Stress

Our western civilisation is a 'thinking' civilisation. We are thinkers, doers, achievers. Life is to be seized (*carpe diem* – 'seize the day'), organised and controlled. We have put a man on the Moon and linked every society in the world with telecommunications. We are proud of our achievements and we push constantly for growth and more growth. But we have had to pay a high price. 'Human beings are the only creatures who spend 99 per cent of their time living inside their own heads,' said Colin Wilson, author of *The Outsider*. We are constantly the victims of our own emotions, swept up and down on an inner switchback. Our minds are never empty of thoughts.

In the East, they call this 'monkey mind' – the daily traffic of sounds going on inside our head, from the minute we get up until the minute we go to bed. It is the endless voice-over running in our mind like a continuous soundtrack superimposed on an endlessly rolling film.

But can we do anything about it?

There is an old story of a Japanese Zen master receiving a visiting student who came to enquire about Zen (meditation). The master served tea. He poured his visitor's cup full, and then kept on pouring. The student watched the cup overflow until he could no longer restrain himself. 'Stop, the cup is overfull. No more will go in.' The master looked at the student and replied, 'Like this cup, you are full of your own opinions and speculations. How can I show you Zen unless you first empty your cup?'

So where to begin?

The only way we can escape from our everyday mind and the pressure of our own thoughts is when we learn to let go, empty our mind – and relax. We need to get out of our mind at least once a day – and turn off and tune in to our own authentic life, our own vibrations and our own inner rhythms.

# Switching off the Pressure

How easy is it to turn off from the inner chatter that is going on in our minds all day long? Let me give you an example. I once attended a meditation course held over a five-day period (two hours each day). There were eight of us on the course, including a family – a husband, his wife and their 16-year-old son. On the first evening we were each given our own mantra (a word sound) to use in our meditation, then asked to go away, meditate that evening and the next day, and return in the evening for a group meditation and discussion. When we arrived, the tutor asked each person to describe what they had experienced during their meditation sessions. When he reached the family, the mother was more than a little embarrassed to admit that when she sat down in a chair to meditate, she fell asleep.

We all laughed. But she went on to say that she couldn't remember the last time she had sat down and really relaxed. She was always looking after the family and doing something for someone else. Dr Chandra Patel, an expert on stress, says: 'A woman can feel out of control because she is constantly attending to the needs of others. While she is busy nurturing others, caring for them and pleasing them, she rarely gets nurtured herself.' This woman had simply let go for the first time in years, and her body had gone into a deep relaxation state followed by sleep. This is not an uncommon experience for someone trying to let go of the everyday mind after years of unrelenting activity. Her problem was only temporary, and she soon learned how to remain relaxed and alert during meditation without falling asleep.

# The Relaxation Response

In the same way that stress triggers a set of biochemical responses, relaxation triggers a set of opposite responses. Harvard professor Herbert Benson called this the relaxation response, after his groundbreaking research into the measurable physical benefits of transcendental meditation (TM). In TM a person is given a mantra – a personal, secret word, sound or phrase – by his instructor. Concentration on this mantra focuses the mind away from the demands of everyday life. It is believed that through its vibration, a mantra has a powerful effect on both the mind and the body. Some meditation schools believe that mantras are ancient Sanskrit sounds handed down by gurus over generations, and that they are personally given by a guru to his disciple.

Endowed with his mantra, the person is then asked to sit in a comfortable position and repeat the mantra over and over again to release all distracting thoughts, and to think about nothing at all. The meditator is asked to do this for 20 minutes every morning and evening.

When Benson monitored several bodily functions of a group engaged in TM, he found:

- a marked decrease in oxygen consumption
- slowing of metabolism
- sharp decrease in blood lactate (associated with muscle tension and physical activity)
- heart rate and respiration slowed down
- skin's resistance to electricity increased (reveals lower levels of tension)
- changes in the nervous and endocrine system
- increase in alpha waves (the slow brain waves associated with relaxation)

In the next step of his experiments, Benson posed the question: 'What if volunteers were taught simple physical relaxation techniques that had no mystical or religious significance to them?' He found that exactly the same response was achieved using any word (not necessarily a special mantra), provided the subject sat in a quiet place and repeated the word over and over for 20 minutes at least twice a day, with the eyes closed and the body in a calm state.

Benson suggested that any word that is pleasing to you can be used – say, 'peace', or 'love' – but he thought that 'one' was a good word, as it is simple and there is a suggestion of unity about it. In a sense, any sound is better than the destructive chatter that normally runs through our minds. So let's give it a try:

1. Find a quiet place where you won't be disturbed for 20 minutes and sit in a comfortable chair that supports your back, or sit cross-legged on the floor (use a cushion for extra comfort), keeping your back straight.

2. Close your eyes. Give yourself a few moments to settle in and you are ready to begin.

3. Begin repeating your word over and over to yourself: 'one ... one ... one.' You can either do this silently or speak the sound quietly to yourself. Another technique is to repeat your word each time you exhale. Try each method to find which you are comfortable with.

4. Adopt a passive attitude – don't worry about how well you are doing. If your mind wanders or you are disturbed by a sound or thought, gently bring your mind back to repeating your word. With practice you will be able to focus for longer periods, increasing your ability to produce the relaxation response. After 20 minutes stop repeating your word and slowly begin to open your eyes.

Simple, isn't it? There is really no great secret attached to the practice of meditation. It can be done anywhere at any time. When you can turn off for 20 minutes without the outside world distracting you, you will be able to meditate on a moving bus or train, in a waiting-room, even in the midst of a noisy football crowd.

Don't worry about special postures. If you are used to sitting in the lotus or half-lotus position, then use it. Or just sit cross-legged on the floor or in any comfortable chair that supports your back. These days, there are a number of specially designed chairs and stools available which support the back in the correct meditation position. Just ensure that your back is kept straight throughout. Poised use of the body prevents fatigue, wear and tear, unnecessary tiredness and aches and pains in muscles and joints.

How long should you meditate for? In the example above we have used 20 minutes, because it can take 15 to 20 minutes to trigger the relaxation response and gain the maximum benefit. But if you are a beginner, start with ten minutes, even five minutes, and gradually increase the time to 20 minutes. The most important gain at this stage is the ability to sit still, turn off, calm your thoughts and tune in to your own rhythm.

## Follow your Own Rhythm

Stress can take a long-term toll on your breathing. When you are stressed you tend to breathe more rapidly and shallowly – hyperventilate – or hold your breath. Your breath tends to go no further than your upper chest. Breathing this way, the oxygen level of your blood drops, the carbon dioxide level takes a jump, and you feel the need to breathe harder.

Oxygen is indispensable to life, and each cell of the body relies on it for fuel. Without an adequate supply of oxygen, cells are starved of the energy necessary to sustain life. Chest-breathing puts strain on the heart since it must pump more blood to carry the same amount of oxygen, and it can lead to increased blood pressure. Efficient (abdominal) breathing provides a rich supply of oxygen to the lungs and hence to the blood and cells; efficient breathing is an important part of feeling good and staying healthy.

Despite the problems you may experience with breathing, you can control the way you breathe and get in touch with the rhythm of your breath. Breathing operates on a conscious and unconscious level: you can notice its flow or you can ignore it. Conscious, calm, abdominal breathing makes you feel instantly calmer. It is the perfect relaxation technique. Taking slow, natural, rhythmic breaths, you can at least double the volume of air you inhale with each breath. Try this exercise. You can practise it no matter where you are or what you are doing:

1. Concentrate, and breathe in through the nose to the count of three.
2. Breathe out as slowly as you can up to a count of six. Your exhalation should be longer than your inhalation. Don't hold your breath at any time. If you find exhaling to a count of six difficult, start with a count of three and increase gradually. Never force your breath and stop if you begin to feel dizzy. As you focus on counting your breath, you will find yourself becoming calmer.
3. While breathing rhythmically, concentrate on raising your abdomen as you inhale and consciously fill your lower, mid and upper lungs with air. To check for abdominal breathing, put your hands on your tummy. It should swell when you breathe in and sink when you breathe out. A good way to master this is to lie on your back in the deep relaxation position (see page 124) and practise until you get the feel of it.
4. Make sure that with every exhalation you let go of all the air you take in. You will get rid of more carbon dioxide and more of the cells' waste products, and you will be able to make use of every new breath of fresh air.
5. Follow your breath in this way for 20 minutes, but if you find that difficult, start with 10 minutes and gradually build to 20. When you have finished, try to remain aware of how it feels to breathe calmly and rhythmically.
6. Brisk walking is an excellent way to develop abdominal breathing. As an aerobic exercise, it demands full use of the lungs.

Use deep breathing any time or place to reduce stress. You will have noticed by now that counting your breath is not unlike repeating a mantra in meditation. You're right. Counting the breath is one of the oldest meditation techniques used in all cultures around the world. It originates from the belief that breath control is the key to the secret of life. In the East it has been practised for more than 2,000 years. In China this vital breath is known as *Chi* or *Qi*, in Japan *Ki*, and in India *Prana*. It is the body's internal vitality and natural healing energy, and its regular stimulation can lead to lasting health and longevity.

Not only do you gain physical benefits from stimulating your vital breath, but you gain mentally and spiritually – you are calmer, more aware and more focused. And this feeling carries over into the rest of your life. Focusing on the rhythm of your breath is one of the easiest ways to acquire a sense of poise and rhythm in your life. It not only revitalises and energises, but it also increases your confidence and self-esteem. It empowers you to cope with the demands of modern life.

Connect with 'the rhythm of life' by using the following seven meditations to help you focus on your mind, breath and body rhythms.

# Awareness Walking

*In order to have peace and joy, you must succeed in having peace with each of your steps. Your steps are the most important thing.*
THICH NHAT HANH

Awareness walking is walking meditation – focusing on the rhythm of the breath and the rhythm of each step to induce a state of deep relaxation and self-awareness. Adding a mind-body technique to walking can provide greater relaxation and stress management, and can turn a routine fitness walk into a creative, rejuvenating experience. Begin by breathing deeply from the abdomen. Let your lungs breathe in their own rhythm. Stay with this feeling for a time, then focus on how many steps you take as your lungs fill and how many steps you take as they empty. If your mind wanders, gently bring your attention back to include both breath and steps. Counting steps and watching the inhalation and exhalation of your lungs helps you touch the basic rhythm of life.

# Movement Meditation

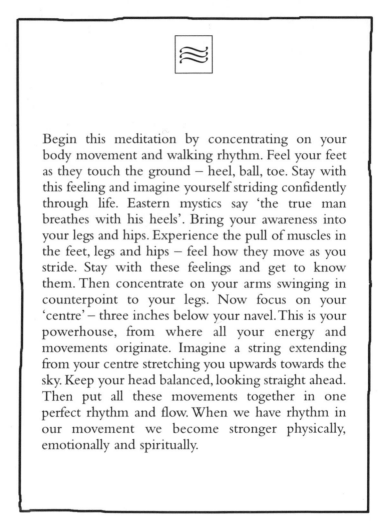

Begin this meditation by concentrating on your body movement and walking rhythm. Feel your feet as they touch the ground – heel, ball, toe. Stay with this feeling and imagine yourself striding confidently through life. Eastern mystics say 'the true man breathes with his heels'. Bring your awareness into your legs and hips. Experience the pull of muscles in the feet, legs and hips – feel how they move as you stride. Stay with these feelings and get to know them. Then concentrate on your arms swinging in counterpoint to your legs. Now focus on your 'centre' – three inches below your navel. This is your powerhouse, from where all your energy and movements originate. Imagine a string extending from your centre stretching you upwards towards the sky. Keep your head balanced, looking straight ahead. Then put all these movements together in one perfect rhythm and flow. When we have rhythm in our movement we become stronger physically, emotionally and spiritually.

# Dance Meditation

We say that a powerful piece of music moves us, and when we move ourselves in tune with music, we dance.

Try this dance meditation. Empty your mind and relax; then put on some favourite rhythmic music and dance. Let go completely – move your body, arms and legs, and let the dance flow; don't force it. Follow it, and allow it to happen. Without thought, without judgement, follow the rhythm and let go of your conscious mind – and just be. Forget yourself and dance until only the dance remains.

In the East, the dervishes are renowned for the mesmeric quality of their whirling, spinning movements when they dance, and the impression of stillness that they convey. It's said that as the dervish spins, his mind is focused on God and upon the awareness that he is turning in complete stillness. Spinning or dancing, the dancer so completely forgets himself that he is lost in the rhythm of the dance and he becomes the dance.

# Discover Walking Mind

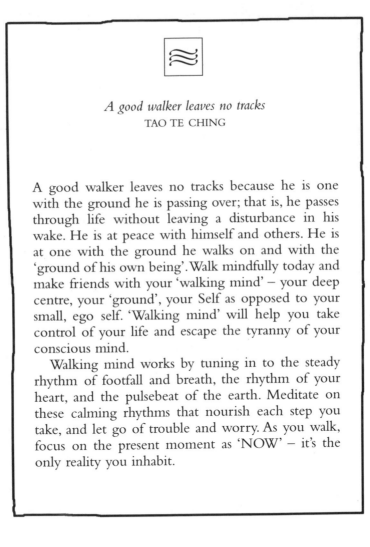

*A good walker leaves no tracks*
TAO TE CHING

A good walker leaves no tracks because he is one with the ground he is passing over; that is, he passes through life without leaving a disturbance in his wake. He is at peace with himself and others. He is at one with the ground he walks on and with the 'ground of his own being'. Walk mindfully today and make friends with your 'walking mind' – your deep centre, your 'ground', your Self as opposed to your small, ego self. 'Walking mind' will help you take control of your life and escape the tyranny of your conscious mind.

Walking mind works by tuning in to the steady rhythm of footfall and breath, the rhythm of your heart, and the pulsebeat of the earth. Meditate on these calming rhythms that nourish each step you take, and let go of trouble and worry. As you walk, focus on the present moment as 'NOW' – it's the only reality you inhabit.

# Expand your Compassion

*The soul of humanity is like a bird with two wings: one wing is wisdom, the other is compassion; the bird will only fly if both wings are in perfect balance.*

Relationships are a major cause of stress – at work, at home, with partners, co-workers, loved ones and children. It's easy to look at life through self-tinted spectacles, seeing only the reflection of our own fears, doubts and anxieties. Pause for a moment today and meditate on the other person's point of view. Do this during a sitting meditation or a mindful walking meditation.

We all see life from a different angle, with its light and shadow side, and we often project our own inadequacies on to others. Step aside today and look at yourself and at others with the eyes of compassion. Meditation reveals and heals. It puts us in touch with our own deepest reality and vulnerability.

# Om

*Meditation is your birthright!*
*It is there, waiting for you to relax a little*
*so it can sing a song, become a dance.*
OSHO

Perhaps the most famous mantra of all is Om. The earliest reference to it is in the Vedic writings called the Upanishads, composed between 800 and 400 BC. It is said that all mantras are hidden in Om. Om is the eternal word, what was, what is and what shall be – the power which orders creation.

The word pronounced Om is broken down into three syllables: A, U, M. A is referred to as waking consciousness, U is dreaming consciousness, and M is sleeping consciousness. The actual pronunciation is 'Oh-Mmm'. Repeat Om aloud, in a whisper, or silently. Feel its vibration all over the body, from the head to the feet. By repeating the mantra, you are charging your breath and energy with the energy of the mantra. The rhythmic vibrations produced have a calming and relaxing effect on the mind, body and spirit.

The Indian classic *Bliss Divine* counsels us to: 'Live in Om. Meditate on Om. Inhale and exhale Om. Rest peacefully in Om. Take shelter in Om.'

# Who Am I?

It is a question we all ask ourselves at some time in our lives. Begin by following your breath, then pose the question: 'Who am I?'

Meditate on this for a while, then ask yourself: 'How old am I?' A teenager might answer 'I am 15 years old'. You or I might say 'I am 45 years old' or '65 years old'. The answer is that we are all 12 billion years old. This is our true age; the age of the universe. And where do we come from? From star-stuff created at the beginning of time itself.

Imagine yourself before the 'big bang', the instant the universe was created. You are contained inside the energy of that moment – we all are. And meditate on this. Then ask yourself another question: 'What was my original face before my mother and father were born?' And meditate upon this. It may not be the answer to the meaning of life, but it gives it some perspective. Personal problems are suddenly brought into sharp relief when we reflect on our true place in the universe.

# The Sixth Way – The Rhythm of Time: Time Management

*Have you also learned that secret from the river;*
*that there is no such thing as time?*
HERMANN HESSE, *SIDDHARTHA*

One of the most frequent complaints from people who are stressed is that they have no time. Worrying about having too little time to do everything you have to do or would like to do is stressful. Yet we all have exactly the same amount of time each day to dispose of – 24 hours, neither more, nor less.

Most of the time we get carried along by time. We are born, grow up, go to school; some of us marry, have children; we all die. We experience life as a river of unceasing events one after another. Like the river, we never stop. We never stop, because there is no time to stop. Time is relentless. There is always something to do. Most of us live in an environment created by others. We exist in a time belonging to others, and our lives are organised and switched on to their plans, their goals, their agendas, their hopes and their desires.

But it doesn't have to be like that. The modern Argentinian writer Borges offers us a different view of time: 'Time is the substance I am made of. Time is a river that sweeps me along, but I am time.'

## Entering the Flow

I like this idea of time. Not the inscrutable vastness of cosmic time back to the 'big bang' and forward into infinite space; not social, experienced time, the clock that is always ticking away, organising our lives around calendars, filofaxes and schedules; but 'inner time', authentic time, a time to be alone, to reflect on who we are as authentic people – where we have come from and where we are going. A time to flow.

Time as we know it didn't exist before the Industrial Revolution. Life moved at a more leisurely pace, with the rhythm of the seasons and the daily rhythms of sunrise and sunset. Then, suddenly, men and women were required to report for work in factories and mines on pain of losing their job if they were late. Everyone needed to follow the same time. Later, the universal synchronisation of time came about with the organisation of transport, as railroads established regional, national and inter-national networks. Everywhere, it was necessary to recognise an agreed standard time.

It was the First World War that saw the increased use of watches to tell the time. Following their issue as standard military equipment, the battle of the Somme began when hundreds of platoon leaders blew their whistles as their synchronised wrist-watches showed that it was 7.30 a.m. Today, the watch is the most-produced object in the world. Everybody has a watch, but no one has time.

It's as well to remember that how you spend your time is how you spend your life. The writer Rabelais said: 'The hours are made for man and not man for the hours!' From time to time we all need to take time out and stand back to look at the larger picture before committing ourselves to goals and objectives. After all, if you don't know where you're going, how can you possibly know when you've arrived? You need to stop at times and take stock. You need to reflect and remember just who you are, because in the headlong rush of modern life, it's so easy to forget. But to remember who you are, you need time. Time to switch off and time to be still. Time to connect with the flow of your own inner rhythms – to become one with the rhythm, with your own heartbeat and with the heartbeat of the earth.

There are many ways to connect with your inner rhythms. One way, which we considered in the previous chapter, is to relax and access your deepest self through meditation. Another way is to organise your time better.

# Know What You Want

To get time under control we need to get ourselves under control. At school no one teaches us how to use time. We are left to get on and muddle through as best we can. Yet what often determines whether one person is more successful than another is the way they use their time. Time is the most democratic resource given to us. Kings, presidents, prime ministers and paupers are all allotted the same amount of time. You can't buy, borrow or steal time – you can only use it. And it's how you perceive it, organise it and use it that determines your ability to master it.

Have you ever wondered where time goes? Consider the time spent by the average UK adult:

- Sleeping: 7 ½ hours per day
- Watching TV: 3 ½ hours per day
- Commuting: 43 min per day
- Eating and snacking: 2 hours 15 min per day
- Playing sports: 30 min per week

Time is what we make it. It is either a precious gift to be nurtured or a millstone we drag around with us. If you allow others to organise your time, you delegate your life to them. This applies as much to someone working at home, trying to balance the demands of a job and looking after a family, as it does to someone working in an office. Under pressure you can lose sight of priorities, allowing certain activities to crowd out others, leaving you harassed, stressed and unable to cope.

In the end, you are either self-programmed or you are programmed by someone else. But by organising your time efficiently, you will be in control of your own life. Success means accomplishing whatever you want out of life, not living up to others' expectations. Successful people set priorities in relation to their own goals rather than someone else's. They:

- learn to plan
- learn to concentrate on the 'important' activities – the activities that make a difference
- learn to screen themselves from unnecessary interruptions
- learn to delegate
- learn to disregard trivia

To make more of your own time, begin by reflecting on and reviewing your priorities and lifestyle.

## Reflection and Review

The first step towards achieving success is working out what will make you, as an individual, feel successful. Spend time thinking about your goals – professional goals, personal goals; major and minor; short-, intermediate- and long-term. As the writer Thoreau said, 'People seldom hit what they do not aim at.' Knowing your goals then becomes your guideline on how to spend your time. If you don't know what you want, how do you know what to do with your time?

Look back over your life. What really mattered? What was important to you? Compare these priorities to how your time is now spent. Make a personal inventory of how you spend your time. Keep a diary for a fortnight and write down in 15- or 30-minute increments all your activities. You will be amazed where your time goes. Is this how you want to continue spending your time, or are there new priorities that you want to consider? Perhaps you're not sure of your goals, in which case try some brainstorming to make them clear. Tap into the rhythms of your intuitive mind with these seven creative ways to record your thoughts, feelings, hopes and desires:

1. **Write them down.** Write your goals down and let your mind soar. Use your imagination and intuition. Capture any idea, no matter how absurd it may seem. Don't be limited by time, money, current skills, past failures – anything. Carry a small pad with you so you don't miss out on those unexpected 'eureka' ideas. Record your dreams and they will become reality.

2. **Fantasise about goals.** Every night for ten nights set down on loose sheets of paper every word that comes into your head over a period of about 20 minutes. Don't read over the pages after they have been written, and don't look at them until after the ten days have finished. Don't be inhibited by beginnings. Damn the torpedoes and just say: 'What I really want is . . .' or 'This is what I think about . . .' Around the fourth or fifth day, obsessive themes may begin to occur. Don't worry, don't edit, and don't

look back – just keep going. Give these thoughts their head. They have tremendous energy – they speak the truth. The conscious, ego mind is suspended and the internal censor, the critical voice lurking in the back of your mind, is silenced. In this state, the words flow like pure water in a running stream. In this flow state, you make associations and connections. If you write wildly without worrying about editing, you will release powerful emotions. Just let go. After the tenth night review your musings. You will be pleasantly surprised.

3. **Tape your goals**. Record your goals on an audio cassette. Try an improvisation in the same way as the writing above. Don't think, don't edit, just begin speaking – 'What I really want to say is . . .' – and go for it. Let it flow. There's nothing holding you back. You can say anything you want. Let your heart and soul cry out their deepest longing. Just record the voice and play it back later, when you can review and reflect on its meaning. Remember to carry your recorder with you to capture those elusive ideas.

4. **Draw a mind map**. A creative way to explore goals on paper is to draw a mind map. It's a more graphic, right-brained, holistic approach than the usual linear way of writing. To begin, draw a circle or oval in the middle of the page to represent an idea you want to explore. From the edge of the circle, draw lines out in any direction to indicate related ideas. Then, from these lines, add subordinate ideas by branching off. Take the mind map as far as you want. You can use different-coloured pens to indicate the main branches. Be creative.

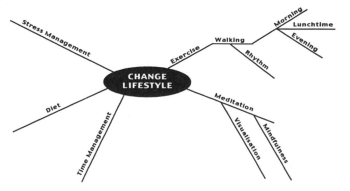

5. **Try 'imagineering'**. The term was coined at the Alcoa Corporation and means 'letting your imagination soar and then engineering it back to earth'. With imagineering, you go over your goals, visualising how things will turn out if they go to plan. Sportsmen use it and public speakers use it, but it must be backed by enthusiasm and determination to make the mental image become reality.

6. **Go for a 'non-thinking walk'**. Use the Zen technique of first thinking about your goals, then putting them out of your mind and leaving the subconscious to do the work. All you do is relax and keep walking. The subconscious goes on in the background churning the problem over, then suddenly, eureka! Everything falls into place, and your goals and the action you need to take are clear to you.

7. **Leave it to the subconscious**. Think about your goals before going to bed, then put them out of your mind and leave the subconscious to do its work. During the night the subconscious will carry on making connections and associations and will integrate all the material you have given it. When you awake in the morning, all will be clear to you.

## Planning and Preparation

Having established your goals, you now have to plan a time frame for them. Goals aren't something you achieve or accomplish. They are something you work towards, usually over a period of time, by doing a series of activities. A simple example is writing a book. The completed book, ready for submission to the publisher, is the goal. To complete the book, one way would be to break it down into a number of activities scheduled over a period of time – chapters and sections. All goals are dependent on a game plan to reach the goal by goal-setting (knowing what you want) and time management (organising your time to get what you want). Success is then a matter of keeping an eye on your goals to help motivate you to complete the activities to achieve them.

Realising your goals becomes a matter of 'What do I do next? Where do I put my energy to realise the greatest possible benefit?'

The key to these questions lies in the following story. In the

1930s there was a very successful executive who felt that he wasn't being as productive as he might be. So he called in one of the management gurus of the day, Ivy Lee, to follow him around for two weeks and observe and note everything he said, everything he did and every piece of paper he tackled. At the end of two weeks he handed a single piece of paper to the executive with three pieces of advice:

- Each day make a 'To do' list.
- Prioritise the activities on the list.
- Tackle the activities in order of decreasing pay-off.

The executive was Charles Schwabb, president of Bethlehem Steel in the USA. Bemused by Lee's succinct advice, he asked him how much he expected to be paid for it. Lee suggested that Schwabb spend one month putting the ideas into practice and then pay him what he considered the ideas were worth. At the end of the month Lee received $25,000 – a lot of money in the 1930s. Charles Schwabb said that it was the best business advice he had ever been given. Today it is still as valuable as it was in the 1930s, and it is the key to successful time management.

Success depends on being prepared, organised and focused on the important tasks that make a difference. Every day ask yourself the question: 'Is what I'm doing moving me closer to my goals?' Then plan and organise your day using this variation on the Charles Schwabb system.

- **Make a 'To do' list**, then prioritise tasks into three categories – A, B and C.

  **A tasks: Urgent and Important** – emergencies, deadlines and short-term goals; tasks that must be done immediately or in the near future; tasks that take precedence over everything else. For example, a piece of vital equipment that has broken down is both urgent and important, because workers may be idle and production may be lost.

  **B tasks: Important but Not Urgent** – goal-setting, planning, exploring new opportunities, relationships, recreation. Examples: taking a course to help you gain promotion, beginning a diet, researching a pension plan, volunteering some of your spare time. These are the tasks which separate effective people from ineffective people. These are the proactive tasks (the tasks that make things happen) as opposed to the reactive tasks ('putting out fires' and being driven by other people's priorities).

**C tasks: Urgent but Not Important** – telephone calls, interruptions, unexpected visitors, mail, some meetings, pressing matters that waste time. Just because something is placed in front of you doesn't mean that you have to give it your immediate attention. These tasks contribute nothing or little to your overall goals.

All other tasks are neither urgent nor important and include such things as trivia, time-wasters and enjoyable/diversionary work (work which gives a feeling of activity and accomplishment but is used as an excuse to put off B tasks which can bring greater benefit).

- **Concentrate on B tasks**. Aim to spend the greatest part of your time on the B tasks (important but not urgent) on your 'To do' list. By focusing on planning, many of the A tasks (emergencies and crises) will be eliminated. Ensure that you allow sufficient time to complete B tasks, which by their nature often demand large chunks of time and are seldom achieved in one attack – a research project, interviewing new employees, planning an exhibition. Keep your feet on the ground by setting realistic time zones for each of these tasks to pre-empt frustration, panic and crises.

- **Review 'To do' list**. At the end of the day, review your 'To do' list and tick off the items that have been achieved. This will give you a feeling of satisfaction and achievement. Any tasks left unticked can be transferred to the following day or left on a 'longer-term list', depending on what the following day demands. Avoid zoning activities to cover every five minutes of the day. Everyone has experienced the annoyance of beginning an important task only to be interrupted with more pressing problems, so allow time for any short-term problems that may occur.

- **Plan 'To do' list**. At the end of each day, plan your 'To do' list for the next day, and review as you begin and end each day. If delayed until morning, more pressing matters tend to dominate the list and it can end up containing only urgent tasks at the expense of important ones. Mentally rehearse the actions and events of the day ahead so you are motivated and prepared. Mental rehearsal of the future is used by sportsmen and by people who want to surpass themselves. Visualise your goals, see them, and see yourself successfully accomplishing them.

- **Follow your own rhythm**. We considered 'circadian rhythms' – biological clocks which regulate such things as mood and body temperature – in the first chapter. To be effective, it's important to follow your own mind and body rhythms. Some people are at their best first thing in the morning, others later in the day. It's no use pushing your mind and body to tackle activities that neither wants to do. Decision-making is especially difficult during low-energy periods. It is far better to schedule tasks when the mind and body are ready – the result will probably be achieved in a much shorter time with half the effort. Many business people set out to 'clear their desks' first thing in the morning, but if the manager's 'personal best time' occurs in the same period, it is time which could be better employed. It is better to leave the routine until later. Learning to listen to your own body rhythms, so that you intimately know your daily peaks and troughs of energy, will enable you to plan and organise your day for maximum benefit.

# PART FOUR

# Maintenance

*In oneself lies the whole world
and if you know how to look and learn,
then the door is there and the key is in your hand.
Nobody on earth can either give you the key
or the door to open, except yourself.*
KRISHNAMURTI, YOU ARE THE WORLD

# The Seventh Way – Managing Stress from Morning to Night

*Say yes to yourself,*
*to what makes you different,*
*to your feelings, your destiny!*
*There is no other way.*
HERMANN HESSE

'Change your thoughts and you change the world,' says a Chinese proverb. 'There is nothing either good or bad, but thinking makes it so,' said William Shakespeare. Change is the basic driving power of life. Without change there is no movement or growth. Like stress, change can motivate and inspire, or it can breed fear, anxiety and uncertainty for the future. Throughout this book we have taken the positive view that change can both motivate and inspire. Saying 'yes' to yourself, today, tomorrow and for the rest of your life, can become a positive addiction. And it can be forever.

When you are in touch with your own inner rhythms, you are in touch with the rhythm of life itself. Suddenly it all makes sense, and everything you do carries more meaning than simply trying to beat stress. It becomes a whole philosophy of life. So after following the first six ways to walk away from stress, and completing the 30-day stress–release plan, you need to organise your life to maintain a low-stress lifestyle.

The seventh way is maintenance: how to maintain a low-stress lifestyle and manage stress from morning to night. You can begin by adapting the 30-day plan and the nutritional information contained in the diet to suit your own needs. Then add to this any of the following stress–management techniques to keep the rhythm flowing.

# Morning

**Morning meditation**. Instead of turning over in the morning when the alarm rings, try a morning meditation. Fifteen minutes' meditation will do you far more good than the extra sleep. Meditation calms and energises and gives you focus for the day. And it gets those all–essential inner rhythms going.

**Wake up and stretch**. When you wake up in the morning, many of the functions controlled by your body's circadian rhythms have only just begun to quicken. Your heart rate is slow, your body temperature is relatively low, your muscles are stiff and your mind is not fully alert. Instead of reaching for a stimulant like a cup of coffee, spend five minutes doing some wake–up stretches to energise and get into a brisk, positive rhythm. When meditating and stretching, do it in that order.

**A matter of life and breath**. If you think about it, your life is measured in the breaths you take. And it's the quality of each breath that determines the quality of your life. A good oxygen supply improves circulation and benefits body functions. Deep breathing calms you down, picks you up and has instant results. So start the day with five minutes of deep breathing for inner calm and focus. Any time during the day when you feel tense and anxious, stop for a moment, centre yourself and take a five-minute breather.

**Eat lots of carbs**. Carbohydrates are good sources of tryptophan, an essential amino acid which is used by the brain to produce serotonin, a feel-good chemical which promotes feelings of calm. Begin the day with a bowl of cereal or porridge (add dried apricots and raisins for extra fibre). Carbohydrates release energy gradually and keep you going longer.

**Walk to win**. The best kinds of exercise for counteracting stress are continuous, rhythmic aerobic activities like walking. So start the day with the most accessible stress-buster of all – get your body rhythms under control before the day starts and you will stride through the day. Take a walking break anytime you feel a little fagged. During the day we carry repressed emotions around with us in our muscle clusters, such as the shoulders and neck. Walking gets the blood circulating, feeding the muscles that are badly affected by stress. Walk to work if it's convenient, or get off the bus or train a few stops earlier and walk the rest of the way.

**Positive self-talk.** We talk to ourselves all the time and much of what we say is negative and damaging, preventing us from living a fulfilled and successful life. Reverse negative thoughts with powerful self-talk such as 'I am healthy, energetic and enthusiastic. I am a winner. I am going for it!'

**Images that heal.** Influence your health and your day with mental imagery. Don't think about the worst things that can happen. Reverse the process and visualise everything turning out well. Spring-clean your mind by putting clean thoughts into it. Once a day visualise the word 'calm' or 'peace' written on a sheet of white paper. Then imagine yourself in a calm, peaceful place such as a garden with flowing water and bright, colourful flowers – a place where you are in control and you can be yourself.

**Lighten up with a laugh.** Give your body a workout each day with a good laugh. Laughing deepens breathing, increases circulation, relaxes muscles and releases endorphins (the body's feel-good chemicals). Even smiling increases blood flow to the brain and sends messages from the face muscles to the emotional centre of the brain to elevate mood.

## Nine to Five

**Organise your time.** Plan ahead by listing daily tasks in order of priority. Set realistic goals, say no to impossible deadlines and finish one task before you move on to the next. Taking five or ten minutes at the end of each day to review the day and plan the next one is one of the most efficient ways to destress your time.

**Stress that motivates**. Don't be negative about stressful situations. Challenging situations often appear stressful, but they also provide opportunities for change and growth. Plan for these situations by focusing on your objectives. Reflect on similar experiences and how you dealt with them, and use positive affirmations to boost your confidence: 'I am in control. I can handle this problem.' Repeat it to yourself several times and focus on it often.

**Posture check**. Good posture suggests to others that you are alert and confident. At least 70 per cent of human communication is non-verbal, so your posture, gestures and movements can be as powerful as words in getting your message across to others. Stand tall and look the world right in the eye – head up, eyes level. When you sit, don't slouch; keep your pelvis straight, your shoulders down and back, your chest up, and stay relaxed. Remember to breathe correctly. Good posture and good breathing go together. Body-mind harmony flows when your body is relaxed and poised and is in step with its own rhythms. When you step out, walking with a relaxed, poised body and a firm, rhythmic stride shows you know where you are going.

**Listen to your body**. Don't wait for stress and tension to build up. Take regular breaks from work, the desk or the computer. Get up, do a few stretches, breathe deeply for a few minutes, or go for a walk. Learning to listen to your body's natural rhythms will forestall stress before it results in tense muscles and devitalising headaches.

**Clear your desk**. There are only four things you can do with a piece of paper that lands on your desk. You can act on it, pass it on to someone else, file it or bin it. So organise your desk, your paperwork and your filing system so you have a clear playing field to tackle the priority work at hand. Clearing your desk will clear your head.

**Think positive**. Turn negative people into positive people. It's easy to pick up other people's moods and emotions which can stay with you all day, sapping your energy and enthusiasm. By keeping cheerful and standing back from the fray, you let the other person take the strain. Reverse negative situations by using positive power-talk: 'I can see what you are saying, but . . .'

**Drink plenty of water**. Stress dehydrates the body. Losing as little as 1 per cent of fluid in your body inhibits the blood's ability to carry oxygen to the brain and stresses the heart. Drinking several glasses of water a day will keep your body supplied with its most important nutrient and it will hydrate away high anxiety.

**Avoid danger foods**. Shun refined carbohydrates such as sugar, in drinks or in processed snacks (they can cause mood swings). Choose fresh, unprocessed foods such as fresh fruit, vegetables, nuts and pulses. And cut down, or better still avoid, caffeine – it can provoke anxiety and depression. Go easy on alcohol. A glass or two with a meal can aid digestion and help you wind down and relax, but too much can destroy essential nutrients and act as a depressant.

**Anger hurts**. Whenever you feel angry, stop and think for a moment about the effect it is having on you. Anger, left unchecked, can be the cause of physical and mental distress. 'When angry, count to ten,' said Thomas Jefferson. And when very angry, count to 20, several times, very slowly. Breathe deeply and relax. A mantra like 'Om' with its long vowel sound can produce the same calming effect.

**Cultivate mindfulness**. Mindfulness is an ancient form of meditation which allows you to meditate anywhere, anytime. As a form of meditation, it requires you to pay attention from moment to moment. It can deliver the same health benefits as TM (transcendental meditation) and it can produce an almost immediate feeling of inner calm. The key to success is a calm awareness of the moment, whether you are working, relaxing or making love. Simply becoming aware of your breathing is a form of mindfulness. Focusing on the moment-to-moment inhalation and exhalation of breath can defuse destructive emotions and strength-sapping tensions.

**Negotiate for what you want**. Your boss does it, his boss does it, we all need to do it. People don't always give us space; we have to negotiate for it, sometimes we have to take it. Don't expect other people to figure out what you need. Communicate it to them. Take the advice of Dr Chester L. Karrass, a leader in the field of negotiation: 'In business you don't get what you deserve, you get what you negotiate.'

**The art of delegation**. Don't try and do everything yourself, either at home or at work. Get someone else to do what you don't have time for by delegating. Can you rely on others to do the job right? The trick is to give clear, complete instructions, and to write them down – what you have delegated, to whom, and when you expect it to be done.

**Learn to say no**. The most effective stress-buster of all. You can't do everything and no one should expect you to. If you find it difficult to say 'no', try assertiveness training.

**Get a grip**. Squeezing something helps to vent stressful emotions and relaxes taut, tense muscles. Keep a hand exerciser or a soft ball in your desk and give it a few squeezes whenever you are tense.

**Take a nap**. Winston Churchill, an enthusiastic advocate of the afternoon nap, said: 'Nature had not intended man to work from eight in the morning until midnight without the refreshment of blessed oblivion which, even if it lasts only 20 minutes, is sufficient to renew all vital forces.' Napping is *de rigueur*. Overworked executives are being encouraged to take a 'power nap' in the afternoon to help them survive the pressure at work. Optimise cat-nap time by keeping it to 30 minutes or less – more than that can interfere with night-time sleep.

**Check out Chi Kung**. An office where sickness and absenteeism isn't a problem – sounds too good to be true? An IT firm in West London, Omni Solutions, is at the forefront in promoting the ethos that a healthy workforce is a happy workforce. Three times a week the employees turn up before work to practise Chi Kung (also known as Chi Gong or Qi Gong). The Chinese have been using Chi Kung as a stress-buster for thousands of years. It is a holistic system which combines breathing techniques with precise movements to stimulate the flow of energy within the body and give an energy boost. Why not ask your own management to provide something similar? You could ask them at least to provide a 'quiet space', a 'meditation room' where employees could relax and unwind for 15 minutes rather than take a coffee break. Sell the idea on the benefits to the company – a healthy workforce and increased productivity.

## Evening and Weekend

**Target your inner soul.** The evening is a time to make time – to pamper yourself a little or a lot. No matter how busy you are, always find time to slow the pace and get in touch with your 'calm centre'. Just five minutes of deep breathing or repeating a mantra will connect you with your inner rhythms and revitalise you for the evening ahead. When you have time, stride out with an energy-boosting brisk walk. Then wind down with some cool-down stretches, deep relaxation and a spirit-enhancing meditation.

**Five-minute massage.** Massage can reduce stress and tension, improve circulation, calm and relax your nervous system, and activate your body's own self-healing mechanisms. And it can take years off you. It works by stimulating blood flow to the body tissues, resulting in better oxygenation and cell nutrition. Give yourself a head or facial massage; better still, let your partner give you one. Lengthen the time with a full-body massage.

**In the swim.** Swimming is another continuous, rhythmic aerobic exercise like walking. It is a quick and easy way to destress, tone up your body and top up your energy all at the same time. Swimming builds stamina, strength and suppleness and uses nearly all the major muscle groups in the body. It's especially good if you're overweight or suffer from backache, because the body is supported in water and there's less risk of injury compared with other exercises.

**Aromatherapy.** Used as a healing technique for thousands of years, aromatherapy uses essential oils to promote and maintain health and encourage deep relaxation. Experiment with popular oils such as lavender, sandalwood, geranium or rosemary. Try ylang

ylang for its calming and aphrodisiac qualities. These stress-busting oils are a good way to head off stress by calming brain chatter. Add essential oils to bath water or a foot bath, use to scent your room, even add to a machine wash for a relaxing smell to your clothes. Smells can influence your emotional state and individual oils can have a therapeutic effect on your body. Essential oils are very potent, and if you want to massage them directly into the skin, they should be mixed with a carrier oil such as almond, soya or grape seed.

**Walktalk therapy**. Freud called his therapeutic technique 'the talking cure'. But you don't need an expensive therapist to listen to you and give you advice. Ask your partner or your best friend. Go for a walk together. The healing power of rhythm unlocks harmful emotions and creates harmony out of discord.

**Family fitness**. According to surveys on family values, many people feel that the greatest threat to their families is the lack of time they spend together. For those looking for something to do with the family that's more meaningful than staring at a TV screen, then lacing up the kids' walking shoes and taking to the outdoors can be a way to strengthen family bonds and family bodies. It's said that the family that walks together talks together. The whole family can get fit and healthy together whilst having a good time. Evenings and weekends can be a time to relax and unwind whilst finding more time for each other.

**Back to nature**. There's something very comforting about knowing that you're connected to the whole of nature. There's that feeling of 'coming home' and 'belonging' when you're in the presence of hills, mountains, rivers, oceans and wildlife. Nature presents us with an opportunity to reawaken the senses. In an urban environment we tend to live mostly in our heads. The great outdoors makes us more mindful, more aware of our surroundings. As we awaken all our senses, we become whole again.

**Pet therapy**. There is evidence that pets can reduce stress. They are a source of constancy in a world of change. They give us companionship, they make us feel safe, and they make us feel calm when we touch them. Caring for a pet can provide a sense of belonging and opportunities for play and entertainment. Animal ownership has been associated with improved health − reduced anxiety, lower blood pressure and a reduction in stress levels.

**Late moods**. An evening walk will help you sleep. A short stroll prior to bedtime releases muscular tension and helps you relax − and sleep comes much easier when the muscles are relaxed. Take Charles Dickens's advice: 'If you can't sleep, try walking.'

# The Way Ahead

Where do we go from here? I would like to finish with a meditation. Life is a continuous flow of change from which we cannot escape. Calmness, harmony, vitality and joy can be attained only if we give in to the natural rhythm of life. To do this we need to be flexible and adaptable. As the ancient Chinese text the Tao Te Ching says, 'Whatever is flexible and flowing will tend to grow; whatever is rigid and blocked will wither and die.' Like a branch bending in the wind, we either cope and flow with the situation, or we crack and break up, at best we remain in a state of stress.

The meditation I want you to consider is on the 'Tao'. It is said that 'the Tao is that whereby all things become complete'. The Tao (pronounced Dow) comes from Taoism, one of the main philosophical systems of China (its main text is the Tao Te Ching), dating back to its founder Lao Tse in the sixth century BC. The Chinese word Tao means 'the flow of nature', 'way', 'road' or 'walk on'. It is said that the Taoist is the one who has learned to let the legs walk by themselves. In other words, he goes with the flow and follows his own inner rhythms. I would like you to muse on this as you walk and meditate.

The Tao is a metaphor for our journey through life; walking is a metaphor for our journey through life. We walk, we follow the Tao, we meditate, we practise mindfulness, and we experience the power and energy of our own rhythms − the awareness, the relaxation and the deep sense of joy and peace.

The Tao is not a destination. The moment you arrive anywhere you limit the distance you might have travelled. The Tao is a journey − a never-ending journey.

# CODA
## On Rhythm

*The stillness in stillness is not the real stillness.*
*Only when there is stillness in movement*
*can the spiritual rhythm appear*
*which pervades heaven and earth.*
TS'AI–KEN T'AN

*See deep enough and you see musically;*
*the heart of nature being everywhere music,*
*if you can only reach it.*
THOMAS CARLYLE

*All art aspires to the condition of music.*
PATER

## On Meditation

*Teach us to care and not to care*
*Teach us to sit still.*
T.S. ELIOT

*When a man can still his senses*
*I call him illumined.*
BHAGAVAD–GITA

*Meditation is not a means to an end.*
*It is both the means and the end.*
KRISHNAMURTI

# On Time

*Time is the great art of man.*
NAPOLEON

*We ought to see ourselves*
*as people who are going to die the next day.*
*It is the time we think we have before us that kills.*
ELSA TRIOLET, FRENCH WRITER

*Time is long enough to whoever takes advantage of it;*
*he who works and thinks stretches its limits.*
VOLTAIRE

# On Walking

*Walking is a land of many paths and no paths,*
*where everyone goes his own way and is right.*
G.M. TREVELYAN

*The beauty is in the walking;*
*we are betrayed by destinations.*
GWYN THOMAS

*If I have a grain of wisdom*
*I walk along the great Tao*
*And only fear to stray.*
LAO TSE

*A Zen master when asked,*
*'What is the Tao?' replied,*
*'Walk on.'*